PRISM OF POETRY

PATHWAYS TO WRITING

Bob Cameron
JoAnne Cameron

Prentice Hall Canada Inc.
Scarborough, Ontario

Canadian Cataloguing in Publication Data
Main entry under title:
Cameron, Bob
     Prism of poetry : pathways to writing

ISBN 0-13-435330-7

1. Poetry – Authorship. 2. Poetics. 3. Canadian
poetry (English).* 4. American poetry. 5. English
poetry. I. Cameron, JoAnne. II. Title.

PN1059. A9C35 1995   808.1   C95-930180-1

Prentice-Hall, Inc., Englewood Cliffs, New Jersey
Prentice-Hall International, Inc., London
Prentice-Hall of Australia, Pty., Ltd., Sydney
Prentice-Hall of India Pvt., Ltd., New Delhi
Prentice-Hall of Japan, Inc., Tokyo
Prentice-Hall of Southeast Asia (PTE) Ltd., Singapore
Editora Prentice-Hall do Brasil Ltda., Rio de Janeiro
Prentice-Hall Hispanoamericana, S.A., Mexico

ISBN 0-13-435330-7

Publisher: Donna MacCallum
Managing Editor: Linda McGuire
Editor: Evelyn Maksimovich
Production Co-ordinators: Gaynor Fitzpatrick and Deborah Starks
Art Director: Bruce Bond
Interior Design: Olena Serbyn
Cover Design: Carole Giguère
Cover Photo: Ron Lowery / Masterfile
Illustrations on pp. 1, 25, 47, 105: Sharon Matthews
Permissions: Angelika Baur
Composition and Typesetting: Arlene Edgar

Printed and bound in Canada by Friesen Printers.
 2 3 4 5 DWF 99 98

Policy Statement
Prentice-Hall Canada Inc., School Division, and the authors of *Prism of Poetry: Pathways to Writing*
are committed to the publication of instructional materials that are as bias-free as possible.
This anthology was evaluated for bias prior to publication.
     The editors and publisher also recognize the importance of appropriate reading levels and have
therefore made every effort to ensure the highest degree of readability in the anthology. The content
has been selected, written, and organized at a level suitable to the intended audience.

Every reasonable effort has been made to find copyright holders for material contained in this book.
The publishers would be pleased to have any errors or omissions brought to their attention.

▶ Shallow Poem

*by **Gerda Mayer***

I've thought of a poem.
I carry it carefully,
nervously, in my head,
like a saucer of milk;
in case I should spill some lines
before I can put it down.

Section 1: Playing with Words

* *(S)* = student poem

TABLE OF CONTENTS

Section 2: Form and Formula

*(S) = student poem

Section 3: Shape and Style

---

* *(S)* = student poem

Section 4: Theme and Theory

---

* *(S)* = student poem

* *(S)* = student poem

REACHING OUT

VISIONS OF REALITY

ACTIVE LIFE

_____

* *(S)* = student poem

The Natural World

Reflections

Social Issues

* *(S)* = student poem

_____

* *(S)* = student poem

This project has been enhanced by the support of many people whose help we would now like to formally acknowledge.

Many thanks to our former students at Parkland School Division No. 70, who always made us feel we were teaching something they valued. Working with them has been an exhilarating experience.

Sincere thanks are also extended to a number of individuals at Prentice Hall Canada Inc. whose contributions to this book have been extensive and with whom we have worked so closely. We owe a special word of gratitude to Evelyn Maksimovich for her enthusiasm and skillful editorial work in the preparation of the manuscript. We would also like to thank Donna MacCallum and Linda McGuire for their pertinent comments and suggestions on contents and organization.

Finally, a word of appreciation to our friends and family for their support and understanding.

We're grateful.

Prentice Hall Canada Inc. wishes to express its sincere appreciation to the following Canadian educators for contributing their time and expertise in reviewing this anthology.

Eleanor E.A. Bjornson, English Teacher, Anne Stevenson Junior Secondary School, District 27, Cariboo Chilcotin, British Columbia

Carol E. Chandler, (Acting) Supervisor of Language Arts, Halifax District School Board, Nova Scotia

Elizabeth Christie, Teacher, Riverside S.S., Windsor Board of Education, Ontario

Richard R.K. Cranston, Teacher, Martensville High School, Saskatchewan Valley, Saskatchewan

Lynn Ibsen, Department Head of English, Exeter High School, Durham Board of Education, Ontario

G. Paul Joy, Chairperson of English, Moderns, and Drama, St. Patrick High School, Lakehead District Separate School Board, Ontario

Lynley MacPherson, Teacher, Cariboo Hill S.S., Burnaby School Board, British Columbia

Carmen Marshall, Curriculum Consultant, Equity Studies Centre, Toronto Board of Education, Ontario

Sheila Mayberry, English Teacher, Governor Simcoe S.S., Lincoln County, Ontario

Marlene Morgan, English Department Head, Moscrop S.S., Burnaby School District #41, British Columbia

Michael O. Nowlan, Teacher (retired), New Brunswick

Don Robertson, English Department Head, Lord Beaverbrook High School, Calgary Public School Board, Alberta

Sheryl Sands, Assistant Head of English, Cedarbrae C.I., Scarborough Board of Education, Ontario

Stefan Sierakowski, Head of English, Lester B. Pearson C.I., Scarborough Board of Education, Ontario

Inclusion of a person in this list does not necessarily indicate endorsement of the text.

ACKNOWLEDGEMENTS

Poems intend to capture one ray of light, one moment in time. That is why poetry, of all the literary genres, is the briefest and most powerful form of expression.

Poetry is a language which communicates thoughts, feelings, and emotions. These aspects of human experience are often the most difficult to express verbally. As a result, poetry has been criticized for being difficult to understand, and has earned a reputation among high school students for being the least popular of literary genres. Recently, however, there have been many indications that poetry is regaining popularity. More and more people are writing poetry, and each year there are more books, magazines, and newspapers publishing poetry. We hope *Prism of Poetry* will help you to discover that writing poetry can be a satisfying and rewarding experience.

Our expectation in developing this book is not that every beginning poet will produce a superior poem. Rather, we want you to experience the creative process by becoming involved in the dynamic act of feeling, thinking, and creating.

In wrestling with some of the same problems encountered by established poets, you will become a more appreciative reader of poetry and of literature. You will discover that a poem must accomplish one of four things:

- It must paint a word picture,
- It must relate an incident,
- It must create a mood, or
- It must convey an idea.

Poetry, however, is more than just self-expression. Quite often it is written for others to read. If you are writing for an audience, there are a number of factors that you might consider when creating your poem:

- Write about topics that are of interest to you.
- Try to be original, to explore your own feelings, to write what you think is true or real.
- Learn a process: a successful way of approaching your writing.
- Acquire the determination to continue writing.
- Always work to improve your poetry. Rewriting is essential.

The activities outlined in *Prism of Poetry* will help you advance as a reader and as a writer of poetry, particularly if you follow the preceding five hints. Above all, however, remember to have fun with poetry. Play with words. Talk about language. Ask questions. Poems come in a variety of forms, express different feelings, and fit many moods. We hope that you will discover—just as the students whose poems are featured in this book discovered—that poetry is one of the most enjoyable and challenging forms of written expression.

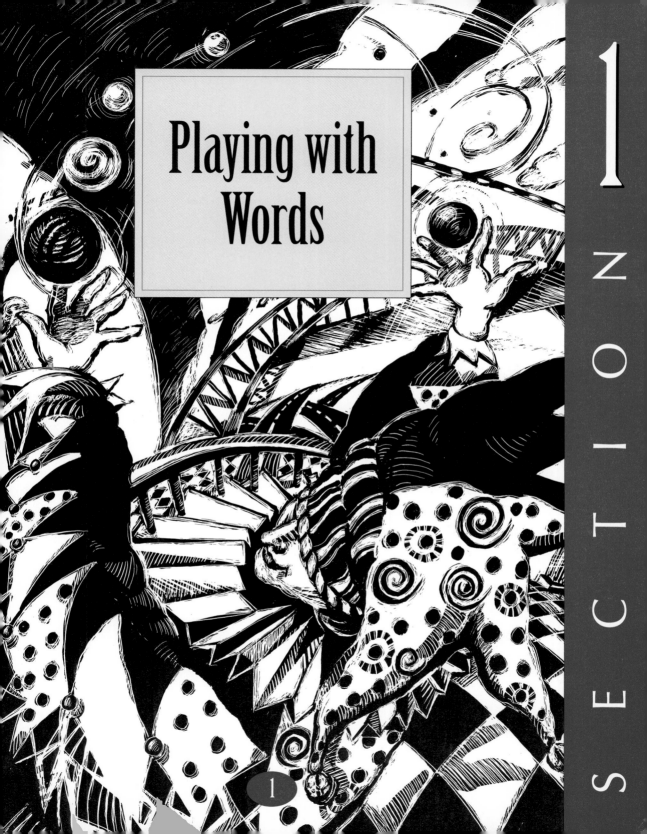

Playing with Words

Adjective Poems

What is poetry? Before you can answer this question, you need to abandon any previously held notions about what poetry is and what it is not. This first section will help you to develop a new perspective on poetry as a form of written expression. By experimenting with words and language in the activities, you will develop a sensitivity and feel for language.

One way to begin exploring poetic language is to experiment with adjectives. Adjectives are words that describe or modify a noun or pronoun. When used effectively, adjectives can add sparkle and life to both our spoken and written language.

What is poetry? Who knows?

Not the rose, but the scent of the rose.

— Eleanor Farjeon

To begin to understand the power of adjectives, imagine trying to describe your favourite movie to a friend using only nouns and verbs. Would your description be exciting and interesting, or would it be tedious and boring? What adjectives would your friend use to describe what she or he has just heard?

The following student poem has been developed using adjectives. First, the author chose a topic. Then, he compiled a list of adjectives that described his topic, using consecutive letters of the alphabet. Because there are very few adjectives beginning with the letter "X," the author chose to substitute an adjective that began with an "X" sound.

▶ Skiing is...

*by **Michael Janzen** (student)*

amazing,

buoyant, captivating,

daring, elevating, fabulous,

gory, hazardous, infectious, jeopardizing,

kinky, locomotive, magnificent, nifty, outrageous,

phenomenal, quick, reckless, sensational,

tremendous, unbelievable, vigorous,

wild, excellent, yielding,

zany!

Notice that this author chose to arrange his list of adjectives in the shape of a diamond, but you can use any format you wish.

It is also possible to use the list of adjectives to compose a more complex poem about the topic. This detailed poem does not have to **rhyme**. It can be developed using as many words from your list as you want, including multiple adjectives beginning with the same letter of the alphabet. The words can also be arranged in any order you choose. The adjective list is simply the focal point of the poem.

As you read the next three examples, try to identify all the different adjectives the authors chose to incorporate into their subject-specific poems.

▶ Super Nintendo

*by **David McGruther** (student)*

Absolute
Best in the world.
Bodacious, Calming
My favourite toy.
Dynamite, Expensive, Fabulous
One of my best purchases.
Graphical, Hip, Immense, Jolly
A w e s o m e   a n d   r a d i c a l .
Keen, Large, Material, Nice, Outrageous
It gives hours of great enjoyment.
Perfect, Questionable, Radical, Super
Totally the peak of performance.
Terrific, Valuable, Wild
Graphics and sound.
Xeno, Zany

Super Nintendo!

Adjective Poems

Friends

by **Aaron Grenier** (student)

Friends are priceless and precious

Friends are youthful
young at heart and lively
they are gallant and dynamic

When things get down they are encouraging and optimistic
uplifting

Although human and imperfect
they are notable and outstanding

They are true and unselfish

They are valuable like gold or silver.

Running Shoes

Anonymous (student)

Running shoes are not just for running.
They are for everyday things.
To wear they are comfortable and relaxing,
to look at—informal and old,
to buy they can be expensive and yearly,
once bought, genuine and valuable.

Running shoes are jumpy and kicky,
battered and discoloured.
The older they get,
the more smelly and moldy.
But they are still loved and treasured,
by
those
who
abuse
them.

Prepare a list of adjectives based on one of the topics listed below, or on a topic of your choice. Then, select the best adjective for each letter of the alphabet and compose a twenty-six word poem starting with an "A" adjective and ending with "Z." For example, the topic word "children" could be described as "active" through to "zippy."

books	cigarettes
teachers	cars
a school subject	principals
pizza	guns
trees	garbage
flowers	dishes
television	movies
jewels	Canada
cookies	a province
fathers	mothers
sisters	brothers
stars	newspapers
computers	grandparents
soap	video games
balloons	a sport

COMPUTER TIP

Instead of trying to think of adjectives in alphabetical order, input all the adjectives you can think of to describe your subject, each word on a separate line. Then highlight your list and use the "sort" command to put your list in alphabetical order.

WRITING FOCUS

A D J E C T I V E S   P L U S

Work with a partner to brainstorm a list of adjectives on a topic of your choice. On your own, write an adjective poem using your list of words. This time, however, compose a more complex poem by experimenting with the alphabetical arrangement of the adjectives, and adding other words and phrases if you feel you need them. Revise and edit your poem with your original partner to ensure you have expressed your feelings about the topic.

Give the poem a title.

Adjective Poems

Display your poem in an attractive way using art materials of your choice. You might design a collage background for your poem, or create a **shape poem** by positioning the words in a way that illustrates your topic. For more information on shape poetry, see pages 63-70.

A poem should not mean
But be.

— Archibald MacLeish

Adjective Poems

Adverb Poems

In the same way that an adjective poem uses adjectives to describe a person, place, or object in a poetic manner, an adverb poem uses adverbs to describe action.

An adverb is a word that modifies or qualifies an adjective, verb, or other adverb, and expresses a relation of time, place, circumstance, manner, and so on. Words such as *gently, so, now, where,* and *why* are all adverbs. Just as an adjective poem is made up of adjectives, an adverb poem consists of lines that begin with an adverb (usually an adverb that ends with "ly"). As the following student samples show, any adverb, or series of adverbs, may be used.

▶ Bicycle Ride

Anonymous *(student)*

Quickly the bike coasts
         down
            the
              hill.
Quickly speed increases; you need skill…
Quickly the front tire blows
Quickly you're sliding, clothes ripping,
Quickly you sense pain, loneliness
Quickly you call for…
            help!

Eagerly

by **Melanie Bubenko** (student)

Eagerly, the skier exits the chairlift;
Eagerly, he allows his skis to cascade
  across the carefully
        p
        a
        c
        k
        e
        d
      snow;
Eagerly, he passes novice skiers—he has
    but one destination—the soaring elevation
    of pure powder.
Eagerly, he thrusts himself forward

              into the endless expanse

                      of snow.

Waiting

*by **Chasidy Karpiuk** (student)*

EAGERLY,
    AWAITING THE ARRIVAL...
        OF A DATE.

NERVOUSLY,
    PRIMPING...
        TO LOOK GOOD.

QUICKLY,
    TRYING ON...
        EVERY OUTFIT YOU OWN.

HAPPILY,
    SATISFIED...
        WITH YOUR LOOKS.

ABRUPTLY,
    THE PHONE...
        RINGS.

SADLY,
    REMEMBERING...THE DATE
        WAS FOR TOMORROW NIGHT!

WRITING FOCUS

A D V E R B   A D V E N T U R E

Write one or two adverb poems on a topic of your choice. Try to choose an adverb (or adverbs) that will complement the **rhythm** and **tone** of your poem. You might consider using one of the following adverbs: slowly, clearly, angrily, lightly.

Adverb Poems

WRITING FOCUS

P A R T N E R S   I N   R H Y M E

With the class divided into two groups ("As" and "Bs"), each "A" student should select a topic from the column on the left while each "B" student selects an adverb from the column on the right. Write your choice on a piece of paper without discussing it with anyone.

Each "A" student should then pair off with a "B" student. Exchange papers and brainstorm ideas for a poem linking the topic with the adverb. Then, work together to write the adverb poem.

Once you are satisfied with your poem, read it to another pair group. You might take turns reading each stanza.

Topic	*Adverb*
brother/sister	viciously
water	recklessly
dating	hungrily
food	sweetly
feathers	callously
pets	sloppily
wind	swiftly
driving/cycling	gladly
cooking	bluntly

SHARING AND PUBLISHING

Read your best adverb poem to a small group. Ask the group members to suggest other adverbs that would work equally well with the subject matter of your poem.

Adverb Poems

Alphabet Poems

a more challenging activity than creating adjective or adverb poems is writing alphabet poems. Like an adjective poem, an alphabet poem uses consecutive letters of the alphabet. The difference is that alphabet poems must form at least one complete thought and make as much sense as possible.

As you will see from the following two sets of alphabetized sentences, this whimsical approach to experimenting with language can produce some rather unusual results. Note the liberties that have been taken with several letters of the alphabet.

A blind cow danced eloquently for Georgetta Hinkerpickle. It jumped krazily, laughing. Modestly, naive Olivia Price quickly ran sideways to Uncle Victor, who x-rayed young Zacharias.

A beautiful cat doggedly examined, feeling glad, her icky jello, knowingly left moldering near. Orest pretty quickly roared, "Stephen, try Uncle Vince's weird, excellent yellow Zephyr."

These alphabetized clusters can now be transferred into a poetic format. You may not appreciate the fun and hard work that goes into creating an alphabet poem until you try to write your own. As you read the following two student samples, imagine what difficulties the authors had to overcome. What techniques might you use to make the writing task a little easier?

Creased

by **Kelly Armstrong** (student)

A badly creased
denim evening fashion gown
has irritated Jessica
Keller—languid &
maltreated.
Nasty, odious
people questioned
removing sloppy, tattered,
unwelcomed vogue.
Welcome exciting
young zaniness!

You May Now Kiss the Bride

by **Kirsty Foot** (student)

A bride curiously darts
effortlessly forward,
glancing hastily.
Imagines joyfully kissing,
loving.
Mentally nervous,
observing people quietly
rejoicing such terrific
unconditional vows.
Welcoming expected years…
zenith.

Alphabet Poems

Write a sentence or two using words that begin with consecutive letters of the alphabet, starting with the letter "A." If you are having difficulty, refer to either a dictionary or a thesaurus. You may use words beginning with "ex" in place of the letter "X" if necessary. Your goal is to create a sentence (or sentences) that are as grammatically correct and natural-sounding as possible.

As an alternative, create your alphabetized sentences by working backwards from the letter "Z."

Once you have completed your sentences, arrange them in the form of a **free-verse** poem. Place your words on the lines in a way that communicates clearly and powerfully to the reader.

WRITING FOCUS

ALPHABET SOUP

Work with a small group of either six or eight students. Place your chairs in a circle and elect one person to record the words each student contributes during the course of this activity.

Working in a clockwise motion from the recorder, the first student should say a word that begins with the letter "A." The next student should add a word that begins with the letter "B," and so on around the circle. To keep the story moving, negotiate a means of timing each student. You might consider devising a regular **rhythm** by clapping your hands and/or snapping your fingers. If a group member cannot contribute a word for the next letter within the time it takes to complete the rhythm, he or she must assume the role of recorder. The activity ends when every group member has had a chance to be the recorder.

Using the recorders' lists of words, write a group alphabet poem. Share your poem with another group or the whole class.

WHAT'S MY TOPIC?

Write a topic on a piece of paper. Be sure to write your name on the paper before folding it and placing it in the container that your teacher is passing around the class. Once everyone has contributed a topic, take turns selecting a topic from the container. If you happen to select the topic you originally contributed, put it back and choose another.

Write an alphabet poem about the topic on your piece of paper. Once you are satisfied with your poem, share it with the person who suggested the topic.

SHARING AND PUBLISHING

Working with a partner, experiment with altering the line breaks in your best alphabet poem. Discuss how the changes affect the meaning and impact of your poem.

The pen is the tongue of the mind.

— Miguel de Cervantes

Alphabet Poems

Acrostic Poems

Lewis Carroll, the author of *Alice's Adventures in Wonderland,* loved word games and puzzles. Occasionally, he would write personalized poems as gifts for the children of his friends. Carroll would use the letters in the child's name to begin each line of the poem. These types of poems were called acrostic poems, after acrostic puzzles.

The word "acrostic" comes from the Greek *akros* meaning "tip" and *stichos* meaning "row." In an acrostic poem, a word is written vertically down the lefthand margin of the paper. Each line then starts with a word beginning with the designated letter.

There are many different ways of writing an acrostic poem. You can use single words or complete sentences, and you can write about yourself or friends and family using either first names or first and last names. Word ideas can come from a dictionary, newspapers, magazines, or other sources.

An acrostic using names can be either a self-portrait in words, like the following two student poems, or a description of another person, like Lewis Carroll's "Ruth" (p. 18).

WRITING FOCUS

W A R M   F U Z Z I E S

Using art materials of your choice, write your first and last name in capitals down the lefthand side of a large piece of paper or bristol board. On direction from the teacher and at timed intervals, go from one work station to the next, writing one nice thing about each person that begins with one of the letters in his or her name.

After you have written a word or line for every person in the class, return to your own work station and read your "Warm Fuzzy." With its complimentary comments, this personalized poem will be nice to look at when it is "one of those days."

COMPUTER TIP

Warm fuzzies and acrostic poems can be created on a computer. Using large, fancy fonts and other appropriate formatting features for the key letters of your subject, print your poem as a poster to display in your classroom or at home.

SHARING AND PUBLISHING

Greeting Card

Design a greeting card for someone by using the person's name in an acrostic name poem.

Yearbook

Submit your school club acrostic poems to the yearbook committee for possible use in the upcoming yearbook.

Opinion Poems

oetry can do much more than simply describe things, actions, or people. As you experiment with writing poetry, you'll find many opportunities to communicate your feelings and opinions.

The following type of poem is a humorous way to express your likes and dislikes. Each poem consists of four lines and follows this format:

a) In the first two lines the reader is provided with clues to the subject of the poem. These lines consist of seven or eight syllables each, and have an obvious **rhythm**; in this case, an unstressed syllable followed by a stressed syllable. There is also a double **rhyme** ("enough of them," "fluff with them") or triple rhyme ("made for it," "paid for it") at the end of each line.

b) The third line is a single noun which identifies the subject.

c) The fourth line is always the same: "I like that stuff!" or "I hate that stuff!"

The following six poems were written by students and follow the formula. Read them several times in order to get a feel for the rhythm and the rhyme. Then, read the poem by Richard Edwards on page 23. Edwards takes this approach to poetry one step further to express his mixed feelings about an animal many people "love to hate."

Silk

by **David McGruther** (student)

Slimy worms are made for it;
Lots of money is paid for it;
Silk,
I like that stuff!

Wool Sweaters

by **Eddie Craven** (student)

I've really had enough of them;
The endless balls of fluff on them;
Wool sweaters,
I hate that stuff!

Hair

by **Kari-Lynn Dougherty** (student)

Sinead O'Connor has none of it;
A St. Bernard has a tonne of it;
Hair,
I like that stuff!

Spiders

by **Kelly Armstrong** (student)

I scream and yell because of them;
Eight fat legs have fuzz on them;
Spiders,
I hate that stuff!

Worms

Anonymous (student)

Slippery noodles resemble them;
Biologists disassemble them;
Worms,
I like that stuff!

Spinach

by **Michael Janzen** (student)

Popeye gets real strong with it;
I don't get along with it;
Spinach,
I hate that stuff!

Snake

*by **Richard Edwards***

I hate the snake
I hate the snake
I hate the way it trails and writhes
And slithers on its belly in the dirty dirt and creeps
I hate the snake
I hate its beady eye that never sleeps.

   I love the snake
   I love the snake
   I love the way it pours and glides
   And esses through the desert and loops necklaces on trees
   I love the snake
   Its zigs and zags, its ins and outs, its ease.

I hate the snake
I hate the snake
I hate its flickering liquorice tongue
Its hide and sneak, its hissiness, its picnic-wrecking spite
I hate its yawn
Its needle fangs, their glitter and their bite.

I love the snake
I love the snake
I love its coiled elastic names
Just listen to them: hamadryad, bandy-bandy, ladder,
Sidewinder, asp
And moccasin and fer de lance and adder

And cascabel
And copperhead
Green mamba, coachwhip, indigo,
So keep your fluffy kittens and your puppy-dogs,
I'll take
The boomslang and
The anaconda. Oh, I love the snake!

POSITIVES AND NEGATIVES

Divide a page of your notebook into two columns and make a list of objects, people, or situations under the headings "Like" and "Hate." Choose one item from each column about which to write a poem. Refer to the student samples on page 22 to ensure your two poems have the correct rhythm and rhyme.

MIXED EMOTIONS

Reread Richard Edwards's poem "The Snake" on page 23. Find a partner and brainstorm a list of topics about which you both have mixed emotions. Work together to write a **free-verse** poem about one of the topics. You do not have to duplicate the format, rhythm, or rhyme of Edwards's poem, but try to identify aspects of the subject that both of you love and hate.

As an alternative, one of you could write the "positive" **stanzas** of the poem while the other concentrates on writing the "negative" stanzas. Then, you could work together to revise the entire poem so that both the positive and negative verses have the same rhythm. Give your poem a title.

SHARING AND PUBLISHING

Display your best opinion poems on a bulletin board or wall for your classmates to read.

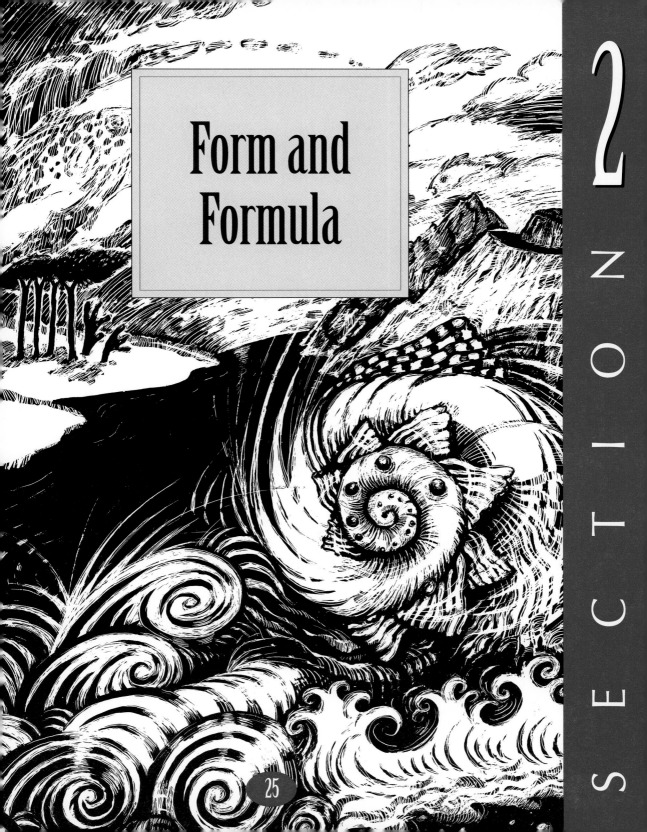

Form and
Formula

Diamante

he **diamante** is a simple diamond-shaped poem that expresses contrast. This poetry pattern was invented by Iris McClellan Tiedt, an American writer, teacher, and librarian. She developed diamantes as a way of allowing her students to express and relate their emotions and ideas in a poetic manner. Tiedt believed that diamantes would give her students opportunities to enjoy the excitement of producing brief, well-stated contrasts.

A diamante may consist of any number of lines, but is usually seven lines in length. It is structured as follows:

- *line one* – one noun
- *line two* – two adjectives describing the noun
- *line three* – three participles (words that end in "ing" or "ed") describing the noun
- *line four* – four nouns related to the subject. (The second two nouns introduce a contrasting idea to that developed in the preceding lines.)
- *line five* – three participles indicating change or development of the subject noun
- *line six* – two adjectives carrying on the idea of change or development
- *line seven* – a noun that contrasts with the noun in the first line

The result is a seven-line contrast poem that has changed in meaning from beginning to end. Read the following diamantes. The first four were written by students.

Coverings

by **Mike Wheeler** (student)

Feathers
Beautiful, colourful
Flying, soaring, gliding
Birds, pillows — ocean-dwellers, snakes
Swimming, slithering, sliming
Slimy, shapely
Scales

Untitled

by **Stephanie Gray** (student)

Summer—
golden, fragrant,
budding, blooming, bursting—
warmth, flowers, youth, brightness—
fading, chilling, shrinking—
pale, dead
Winter.

Friends/Enemies

by **Jonathan Bauer** (student)

Friends
Loyal, sympathetic
Understanding, caring, loving
Companions, chums — opponents, foes
Degrading, despising, distrusting
Antagonistic, bitter
Enemies

Diamante

Diamante

by *Lisa Nicole Anthony* (student)

Rookie

Scared, Unsure

Wondering, Anticipating, Trying

Silly, Amateur — Mature, Professional

Learning, Achieving, Gaining

Sure, Ready

Graduate

Galaxies/Atoms

Anonymous

Galaxies —

Distant, huge

Glowing, turning, going

Space, mystery — energy, life

Growing, circling, building

Tiny, basic

Atoms.

COMPARISONS AND CONTRASTS

In a small group, list a number of people, places, or objects that may be compared and contrasted. For example:

- heavy metal and country music
- winter and summer
- breakfast and dinner
- cats and dogs
- earth and sky
- ballet and football

Working on your own, choose one of the topics from your group's list and organize several points for comparison. Write a first draft of your diamante, referring to the structure outlined on page 27. Ask one of your group members for feedback. Revise your diamante based on your peer editor's comments, then share it with the rest of the group.

> ### COMPUTER TIP
>
> Use your imagination to create a computer-generated diamante. Experiment with the graphics features, such as lines and borders, to create a diamond shape in which you could position your diamante. Or, you might input four diamantes on one page so that together, they form a larger diamond shape.

SHARING AND PUBLISHING

Display
Choose your best diamante and design a way to display it. You might consider using triangular sheets of coloured paper that, when joined together, create the shape of a diamond. Or, you might arrange a thematically-appropriate collage around your diamante.

Choral Reading
With a partner, perform a choral reading of your favourite diamante for the class. One of you could begin by reading the first three lines, then both of you could read the middle line together. Your partner could finish by reading the words after the middle line.

Diamante

Cinquain

t he **cinquain** is a type of short poem invented by an American poet who had studied Japanese **haiku.** The poem consists of five lines of words for a total of twenty-two syllables. The first line has two syllables, the second line has four, the third line has six, the fourth line has eight, and the final line has two. The two-syllable topic line introduces the poem, and the two-syllable ending gives the poem its impact.

When writing poems that have a specified number of syllables, like cinquain, you will find that a great deal can be said in a few words. The words, however, must be chosen carefully, and must contain the correct number of syllables. The lines, which are usually unrhymed, run on. Heavy punctuation marks at the ends of the lines are unnecessary.

Writing cinquain is a logical first step to writing haiku, a more complicated poetic form (see pp. 35-38). After you have read the following cinquain, count the number of syllables in each line.

Rain Drops

*by **Deni-Lee Merritt** (student)*

Rain drops
Clear, watery.
Falling in a rhythm,
Leaving a freshness in the air.
Dew-like.

The Trees

*by **Jane Alden** (student)*

I saw
Two old oak trees
Playing with a ball. One
Threw it in the other's branches
And laughed.

Cinquain

*by **Scott Hennig** (student)*

At night
It's very dark
Highway lights shine brightly
Snow falls ever so quietly
At night

Similarities

Anonymous

I touch

Two curving things:

The barrel of this pen,

The slow uncertain windings of

This verse.

WRITING FOCUS

C I N Q U A I N

Write two or three cinquain on a topic (or topics) of your choice. You might consider topics such as: a season; an animal; an experience with nature; a favourite movie or musical group; a unique (or funny) aspect of your school; your favourite day of the year; graduation; a hobby. Be sure to retain the correct syllable count for each line, and try to select words that are meaningful and have a strong impact.

WRITING FOCUS

T W O   F O R   T W E N T Y - T W O

Work with a partner to develop a cinquain about a national or local event. Scan newspapers and listen to radio and television news broadcasts for ideas. Take note of the words used by the journalists to describe the event. Then, using your notes, select appropriate words to develop your cinquain.

Exchange one of your cinquain with a partner. Try to substitute his or her word choices with other words that have the same syllable count and a similar meaning. Compare the results of the changes together. Then, work on your own to create a final cinquain on the same subject that uses a combination of the words from your original poem and your partner's rewrite. Mount all three cinquain on a picture of your topic and display it in your classroom.

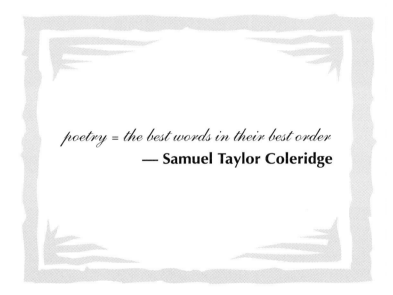

poetry = the best words in their best order
— Samuel Taylor Coleridge

Haiku

The **haiku** poem is of Japanese origin. In its most traditional form, a haiku consists of three lines totaling seventeen syllables. Like a snapshot in words, a traditional haiku represents the poet's impression of an object or scene in nature. The first line, which usually consists of five syllables, contains the setting; the second line of seven syllables conveys an action; the third line, made up of five syllables, completes the thought.

There are many misconceptions about this form of poetry. One misconception is that a haiku must follow the seventeen syllable formula. Traditional Japanese poets, however, counted sounds rather than syllables, and these sounds translate into shorter lines in English. For this reason, many contemporary poets do not concentrate on counting syllables, but they do strive to make each line as succinct as possible.

Haiku focus on one element and are always written in the present tense. A haiku should leave the reader thinking. It should provide him or her with not only a scene, but also an insight.

Calvin and Hobbes

by Bill Watterson

TWITCHING TUFTED TAIL,
A TOASTY, TAWNY TUMMY:
A TIRED TIGER.

...AN ALLITERATIVE HAIKU
BY CALVIN. THANK YOU,
THANK YOU.

SHEESH.

© 1990 Universal Press Syndicate

▶ The Brook

*by **Shauna Soice** (student)*

Softly whispering,
bubbling over with joy,
winding down the hills.

▶ The Dragon Morning

*by **Samir Khalil** (student)*

Clouds of dragon mists
fly in gold of morning sun
dive into the sea

▶ Disappearing Forests

*by **Mike Schneider** (student)*

The sound of the saw,
As the great giants fall down.
To be seen no more.

▶ Shadows

*by **Shiki***

Shadows of the trees:
my shadow wavers with them
in the winter moonlight.

▶ Haiku

*by **Mary Partridge***

August afternoon
bleached snowfencing leans into
a drift of daisies

▶ Haiku

*by **M.J.R. Smith***

on wet crumpled sand
lies a pink glistening shell
waiting to be heard

Haiku

Moss-hung Trees

by **Winona Baker**

moss-hung trees
a deer moves into
the hunter's silence

Long Beach: February

by **Myra Cohn Livingston**

Even the moon lies
on its back, rolling over
to stare into space.

WRITING FOCUS

A S T A R T E R K I T

Think of a subject for a haiku. See if you can brainstorm ideas and **images** that come to mind when you think of this subject. Experiment with words (sounds and syllables) that relate to the subject. Write a haiku based on one of your ideas. If possible, try to observe the five-seven-five syllable formula. Ask for feedback from a peer editor once you are satisfied with your poem.

The following ideas may give you some inspiration for writing your own haiku:

- snow/sugar
- sea/sky
- leaf/death
- tree/broom
- bees/stars
- waves/fingers

Haiku

S E T T I N G ,   S U B J E C T ,   S T A T E M E N T

Work with a small group and choose a setting in nature: a season, a time of day, a place, and/or a month of the year. Decide on a subject that could be introduced in the second line that would emphasize action, such as a mammal, an insect, or some other living (or moving) thing. Then, negotiate what statement or conclusion your group would like to make in the last line.

Once you have settled on the elements of your haiku, work together to write it. Be sure to add an appropriate title.

WRITING FOCUS

A   M O M E N T   I N   T I M E

Scan old calendars and magazines and select an appropriate landscape picture or nature scene. Or, go outside or look out your classroom window and make a mental picture of what you see. Write a haiku based on this image. If possible, display your haiku alongside the picture which inspired it. You may have to draw or photograph your outdoor scene for this purpose.

SHARING AND PUBLISHING

Select three or four of your own haiku that you particularly like. Arrange these haiku on a large sheet of blank paper and illustrate each poem in a manner consistent with the **mood** and words. Display your work in the classroom.

Haiku

Tanka

Like the **haiku** (see pp. 35-38), the **tanka** is a type of Japanese poem that is more than a thousand years old. It consists of five lines (a haiku has three) which contain a total of thirty-one syllables: line one is five syllables in length, line two is seven, line three is five, line four is seven, and line five is seven.

With the additional two lines, the tanka conveys an insight beyond that of a haiku's single moment. The tanka writer has more room to complete his or her thought and/or link it with something else. A tanka may show a progression of ideas or events; a series of tanka related to a central **theme** or time period can be joined together to form a longer poem. Since there are restrictions regarding the number of syllables in each line with the tanka as well as with the **cinquain** and the haiku, words must be chosen carefully. The following three tanka were written by students.

▶ Tree

*by **Dominic Dowell** (student)*

Swaying in the wind
I catch people's attention.
I begin to wave,
They never wave back to me.
I think nobody likes me.

Singing

*by **Matthew Festenstein** (student)*

I'm singing my song,
The words slipping through my lips
Meet their waiting ears,
Then fall into memory
To be whistled out again.

Untitled

*by **Christian Tattersfield** (student)*

Across I travel,
Desolate and cold it is.
My shadow follows.
Just whistling to pass the time—
It helps when you're so lonely.

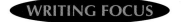

WRITING FOCUS

M E M O R I E S

Recall a personal or imagined experience that you have had. Write notes based on your memories of the experience. Think of a way to position your thoughts on each of the five lines, then select your words according to the syllabic rules governing the tanka. Revise your tanka and give it an appropriate title.

Tanka

Occasionally, poets will string together several tanka in order to form a longer poem. Each tanka represents a separate **stanza** in the poem.

Work with a small group to write several tanka that, when joined together, form a complete thought or lend greater insight into the subject of the poem. Your topic could be a character or literary work that you have recently studied in class, a well-known athlete, politician, or movie celebrity, or a special event in your school or community, and so on. Share your tanka with another group and ask them for their suggestions for an interesting title.

SHARING AND PUBLISHING

Share the tanka you have written during the course of this unit with a small group. As a group, choose one tanka that everyone agrees is the best example of the **form.** Work together to create a series of tableaux that illustrate the thoughts, feelings, and **images** expressed in the tanka. Perform your tableaux for another group or the whole class.

Tanka

Like a piece of ice on a hot stove the poem must ride on its own melting.
— **Robert Frost**

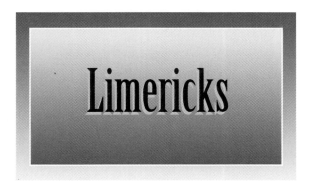

Limericks

Limericks are humorous nonsense poems that have been popular for centuries. The limerick poem consists of five lines that are highly rhythmical and fast-paced. The first, second, and fifth lines **rhyme** with one another, and consist of three distinct beats; that is, each line contains nine syllables. The third and fourth lines rhyme with each other, and consist of two beats (or five syllables). It should be noted, however, that not all limericks follow the nine and five syllable formula. Ideally, the final line should not be simply a repetition or variation of the first line. Instead, it should be witty and act as a "punch line" for the poem.

The ideas in a limerick often progress from the possible to the impossible, drawing attention to real or imaginary situations, people, and places. Fun to write and even more fun to read, the main purpose of a limerick is to entertain.

No matter how grouchy you're feeling,
You'll find that a limerick is healing.
It grows in a wreath
All around the front teeth,
Thus preserving the face from congealing.

— Anonymous

The Ichthyosaurus

*by **Isabel Frances Bellows***

There once was an Ichthyosaurus,
Who lived when the earth was all porous,
But he fainted with shame
When he first heard his name,
And departed a long time before us.

The Panda

*by **William Jay Smith***

A lady who lived in Uganda
Was outrageously fond of her Panda:
With her Chinchilla Cat,
It ate grasshopper fat
On an air-conditioned veranda.

Untitled

*by **Arthur Buller***

There was a young lady named Bright,
Whose speed was far faster than light;
She set out one day
In a relative way,
And returned home the previous night.

Untitled

Anonymous

There once was a gnu in the zoo
Who tired of the same daily view.
To seek a new sight
He stole out one night,
And where he went gnobody gnu.

... Her gown, brocaded, edged in purple

AURPLE, BURPLE, CURPLE, DURPLE, EURPLE, FURPLE, GURPLE, HURPLE, IURPLE, JURPLE, KURPLE, LURPLE, MURPLE, NURPLE, OURPLE, QURPLE, RURPLE, SURPLE, TURPLE, UURPLE, VURPLE, WURPLE, XURPLE, YURPLE, ZURPLE.

... Her gown, brocaded, edged in ~~purple~~ green
Was the prettiest darn gown I'd ever seen.

WRITING FOCUS

GROUP LIMERICK

Try composing limericks as a group. Have each person in your group write a first line that would be suitable for a limerick. Put all the first lines into a container. Have one group member choose a line other than his or her own. He or she must supply the second line of the limerick, then choose a student to contribute the third line, and so on until the poem is finished.

Begin with a new line and start a new limerick, giving each student a chance to contribute. Be sure to keep a written version of all the limericks.

Limericks

GEOGRAPHICAL PROPORTIONS

Work with a partner and scan an atlas of the world for interesting names of capital cities. Choose one name and work together to research the population, local industries, and points of interest about your locale. Take the research notes and, working separately, write a limerick about the city. Try to mix fact with fiction in your poem. Meet with your partner once again and compare the results.

WRITING FOCUS

IN SUMMARY

Choose a recent news article, sports or entertainment piece, or weather report and rewrite it in the form of a limerick. Or, try summarizing your favourite movie, short story, or novel in limerick form.

SHARING AND PUBLISHING

Select your best limerick for publishing in a class anthology. With your limerick, submit a title idea for the anthology and work with your classmates to vote on the best title.

COMPUTER TIP

You may want to use computerized "clip art" images to illustrate your class anthology of poems.

Limericks

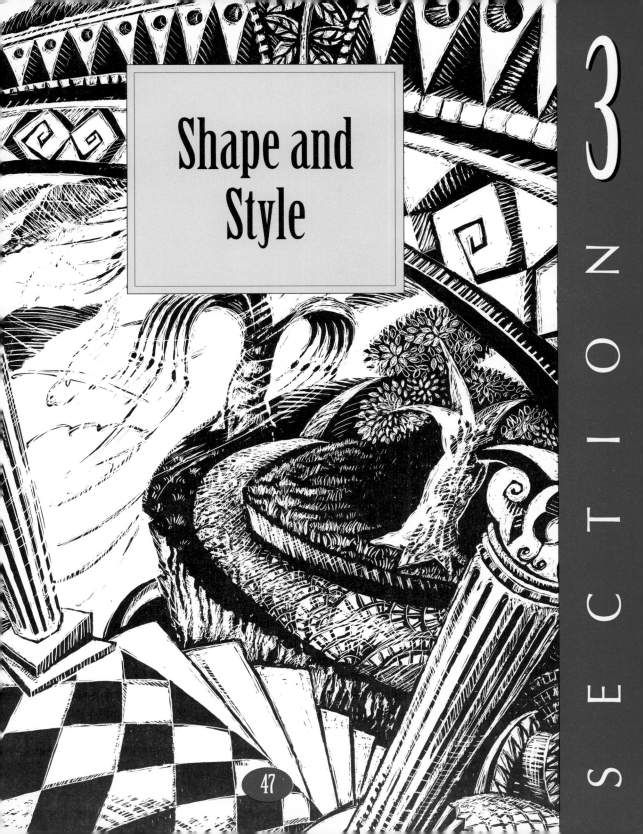

Shape and Style

"What If...?" Poems

everyone likes to dream. In fact, many novelists and poets begin their works of imagination by completing a statement like "I wish…" or "What if…?" Authors of fantasy and science fiction literature, for example, often ask themselves what would happen if one or more aspects of modern life were changed. Then, they write about the ways those changes might affect the present or future world. They compose their stories by asking and answering the question "what if?"

Although imaginative fiction is clearly based on life, the following poems illustrate the kinds of ideas and conclusions poets think about when they explore the realm of life's fantastic possibilities.

THE FAR SIDE   By GARY LARSON

Edgar Allan Poe in a moment of writer's block.

I Wish I May, I Wish I Might

by **Andrew Ford** (student)

I wish I may, I wish I might,
I wish for a Corvette black as night,
I wish for goal pads, white and red,
I also wish for a new waterbed.

I wish I had money,
Tons of gold.
I wish to stay young,
And never get old.

I wish for a dream house,
By the sea,
And a whole new wardrobe,
Just for me!

I wish for boats,
And 100 pound fishes.
But what I want most,
is 1000 more wishes.

I Wish...

by **Yvonne Mik** (student)

I wish I were an only child—
then, no more babysitting of brothers & sisters,
then my parents would spend money on ME,
then I wouldn't trip over their junk,
then I'd get all the attention
then I wouldn't have to be an example for anybody,
I would have a happy life!
then again—
I couldn't live without them.

My Deaf Brother

by **Phebe Graham** (student)

If my brother hadn't been born deaf,
    my world would not be the same.
His world would not be the same,
    if my brother hadn't been born deaf.

If my brother hadn't been born deaf,
        the way the world communicated with him
        wouldn't be the same.
The way he communicated with the world
        wouldn't be the same.
        if my brother hadn't been born deaf.

If my brother hadn't been born deaf,
        the way the world looked upon him
        would be different.
The way he looked at the world
        would be different
        if my brother hadn't been born deaf.

What We Might Be, What We Are

by **X.J. Kennedy**

If you were a scoop of vanilla
And I were the cone where you sat,
If you were a slowly pitched baseball
And I were the swing of a bat,

If you were a shiny new fishhook
And I were a bucket of worms,
If we were a pin and a pincushion,
We might be on intimate terms.

If you were a plate of spaghetti
And I were your piping-hot sauce,
We'd not even need to write letters
To put our affection across.

But you're just a piece of red ribbon
In the beard of a Balinese goat
And I'm a New Jersey mosquito.
I guess we'll stay slightly remote.

If a Poem Could Walk

by **Lorna Crozier**

It would have paws, not feet,
four of them
to sink into the moss
when humans blunder up the path.

Or hooves, small ones,
leaving half-moons in the sand.
Something to make you stop
                     and wonder
what kind of animal this is,
where it came from, where it's going.

It draws nearest when you are most alone.
You lay red plums on your blanket,
a glass of cool cider, two sugar cubes,

knowing it is tame and wild —
the perfect animal —
knowing it will stop for nothing
as it walks
          with its four new legs
right off the page

"What If ...?" Poems

What If?

by **Les Parsons**

What if roads were made of rubber,
Would cars bounce around the block?
And if turtles went to college,
Would they soon learn how to talk?

What if worms wore plastic sneakers,
Would they wear them to a dance?
And if chickens wore suspenders,
Would they lay eggs dressed in pants?

What if clouds were chocolate ice cream,
And what if rain was soda pop,
Would children then love rainy days
And wish they'd never stop?

WRITING FOCUS

F A N T A S T I C   P O S S I B I L I T I E S

Scan your journal for places where you used phrases such as "I wish…" or "what if…?" Make a list of the objects, relationships, or circumstances you wanted to change.

Write a poem in which one or more lines begin with one of the following phrases:

- I wish…
- I remember…
- In the middle of the night…
- I used to be… But now I'm…
- In the past they… But now they…
- I used to like… But now…
- If…

S C I E N C E   F I C T I O N

In a small group, discuss any science fiction or fantasy novels that you have read or movies that you have seen. What questions or circumstances might have initiated the idea for the novel or movie? What ideas and/or consequences was the author trying to explore? What message did she or he leave with the reader/audience at the end of the piece?

Choose one of the novels or movies discussed and write a group "What if…?" poem outlining the questions and answers the author was exploring.

SHARING AND PUBLISHING

Choose one of your "I Wish…" or "What If…?" poems and rewrite it in the **form** of a **monologue.** Read your monologue several times until you feel comfortable enough to deliver it to at least one other person in your class. Remember, monologues express the speaker's inner feelings, attitudes, and reactions toward someone or something else.

Ask your partner to give you feedback on the following: development and expression of ideas; oral skills such as voice control, enunciation, tone, and volume; ability to hold the listeners' attention; body language. Continue to revise and practise your monologue until you feel confident to deliver it in front of a small group or the entire class.

"What If …?" Poems

List Poems

You are a collector of many different kinds of experiences. You store these experiences as memories and access them when you need them. Like other writers, you can draw on this rich resource of remembered experiences when you write poetry. Even simple, everyday actions such as getting dressed, riding the bus, cleaning out a closet, or playing a sport have the potential to become a poem. When these collected experiences are joined together in poetic form, the poem resembles a list.

Some poems simply list objects that have special significance to the authors. Other poems describe the author's insights into his or her experiences.

Like peering through a window, the following list poems provide you with an intimate glimpse into the everyday thoughts and lives of the authors.

Poetry can do a hundred and one things:

delight, sadden, disturb, amuse, instruct. . . .

— W.H. Auden

Grey

by **Cynthia Lim** (student)

How appropriate that
so many things in our
everyday lives should be
that colour (whitish black or
blackish white, even
sooty white, misty black,
a nice ambiguous shade of haze).
Dust, fog, roads of all kinds,
creatures from elephants to mice,
dingy socks, ancient kleenex,
television screens, newspaper photos and
    Poirot's little brain cells.

What in the name of Crayola
convinced Mother Nature to favour
a happy medium
sooty mist or snowy slate or whatever,
over 119 other well-defined shades and hues
plus a dandelion-yellow sharpener?
The answer to this conundrum may only be found
shrouded in
         a cloak of
            grey.

Yes

by **Adrian Mitchell**

A smile says: Yes.
A heart says: Blood.
When the rain says: Drink.
The earth says: Mud.

The kangaroo says: Trampoline.
Giraffes say: Tree.
A bus says: Us,
While a car says: Me.

Lemon trees say: Lemons.
A jug says: Lemonade.

The villain says: You're wonderful,
The hero: I'm afraid.

The forest says: Hide and Seek.
The grass says: Green and Grow.
The railway says: Maybe.
The prison says: No.

The millionaire says: Take.
The beggar says: Give.
The soldier cries: Mother!
The baby sings: Live.

The river says: Come with me.
The moon says: Bless.
The stars say: Enjoy the light.
The sun says: Yes.

THE FAR SIDE   By GARY LARSON

© 1985 FarWorks, Inc./Dist. by Universal Press Syndicate

List Poems

Letter to Milwaukee

(an excerpt)   by ***Roger Mitchell***

The empty stapler, the unsharpened pencil,
the dry rubberstamp of a dead executive,
instructions for the care of lenses,
the closed pipe case, recipes for soap,
unanswered letters from Puerto Rico,
back issues still in plain brown wrappers,
bookmarks stuck into slanted texts
like flags in the sides of whales
hunted by other men in another time.

Jamaica Market

by ***Agnes Maxwell-Hall***

Honey, pepper, leaf-green limes,
Pagan fruit whose names are rhymes,
Mangoes, breadfruit, ginger-roots
Granadillas, bamboo shoots,
Cho-cho, ackees, tangerines,
Lemons, purple Congo-Beans,
Sugar, okras, folanuts,
Citrons, hairy coconuts,
Fish, tobacco, native hats,
Golden bananas, woven mats,
Plantain, wild-thyme, pallid leeks,
Pigeons with their scarlet beaks,
Oranges and saffron yams,
Baskets, ruby guava jams,
Turtles, goat-skins, cinnamon,
Allspice, conch-shells, golden rum.
Black skins, babel — The sun
That burns all colours into one.

A Boy's Head

by **Miroslav Holub**

In it there is a space-ship
and a project
for doing away with piano lessons.

And there is
Noah's ark.
which shall be first.

And there is
an entirely new bird,
an entirely new hare,
an entirely new bumble-bee.

There is a river
that flows upwards.

There is a multiplication table.

There is anti-matter.

And it just cannot be trimmed.

I believe
that only what cannot be trimmed
is a head

There is much promise
in the circumstance
that so many people have heads.

The Credo

by **Robert Fulghum**

All I really need to know
about how to live and what to do and how to be
I learned in kindergarten.
Wisdom was not at the top of the graduate-school mountain,
but there in the sandpile at Sunday School.
These are the things I learned:

Share everything.
Play fair.
Don't hit people.
Put things back where you found them.
Clean up your own mess.
Don't take things that aren't yours.
Say you're sorry when you hurt somebody.
Wash your hands before you eat.
Flush.
Warm cookies and cold milk are good for you.

List Poems

Live a balanced life—
learn some and think some
and draw and paint and sing and dance and play
and work every day some.

Take a nap every afternoon.

When you go out into the world,
watch out for traffic,
hold hands,
and stick together.

Be aware of wonder.
Remember the little seed in the Styrofoam cup:
The roots go down and the plant goes up
and nobody really knows how or why,
but we are all like that.
Goldfish and hamsters and white mice
and even the little seed in the Styrofoam cup—they all die.
So do we.

And then remember the Dick-and-Jane books
and the first word you learned—
the biggest word of all—LOOK.

Everything you need to know is in there somewhere.
The Golden Rule and love and basic sanitation.
Ecology and politics and equality and sane living.

Think what a better world it would be if
we all—the whole world—
had cookies and milk about three o'clock every afternoon
and then lay down with our blankies for a nap.
Or if all governments had as a basic policy
to always put things back where they found them
and to clean up their own mess.

And it is still true,
no matter how old you are—
when you go out into the world,
it is best to hold hands and stick together.

TWO   POEMS

As you may have guessed, Roger Mitchell, in his poem "Letter to Milwaukee" (p. 58), chose to list the items on his desk, including a copy of Herman Melville's epic novel *Moby Dick* which, in an explanatory note, Mitchell indicated he was reading at the time.

Write a list poem about one of the following: the contents of your locker, the cafeteria at lunch, the school hallways at 8:50 a.m., or the contents of something else that is very familiar to you.

Alternatively, similar to "The Credo" (pp. 59-60), you might write a list poem about the "rules" (spoken or implied) that you had to follow when you were little.

WRITING FOCUS

FROM   STORY   TO   POEM

Bring an object to class that has an interesting history, a *story* to tell. The object may be beautiful, mysterious, or ordinary, and the story behind it may be romantic, strange, magical, or frightening. Your role is to talk about the object's fascinating history while it is being passed around to your classmates.

> ### COMPUTER TIP
>
> To make your polished work more attractive, experiment with the various font styles available on your wordprocessing software.

As a listener, your role is to choose five of the objects and make notes about them during your classmates' story-telling. Once the storytelling is finished, work on your own to write a list poem incorporating details about each of the five objects and their corresponding stories. If you have any further questions about the objects and their stories, ask the appropriate storytellers.

Once you are satisfied with your list poem, compare it with the poems of other classmates who wrote about some of the same objects.

List Poems

WRITING FOCUS

T A K E   Y O U R   P I C K

In a small group, brainstorm aspects of several of the topics listed below. Listen carefully to the other group members' contributions.

- "Twenty-five Things That Are Blue" (or any colour)
- "Things That I Will Never Throw Away"
- "Things That I Will Never Forget About School"
- "Reasons Why I'm a Junk Food Junkie" (or "Health Food Fanatic")
- "Things That Make Me Go 'Hmm'"

Write a group list poem based on one of the topics discussed during the brainstorming. Be sure to use the technique of listing things.

SHARING AND PUBLISHING

Create a visual to accompany your list poem. You might consider a collage of pictures, or a video comprised of brief shots of the details outlined in the poem. Be sure to do a voice-over of your poem to accompany the shots on the video.

List Poems

Shape Poems

guillaume Apollinaire (1880-1918) is credited with inventing the **calligram** or **shape poem.** A shape poem is a poem whose typographical arrangement forms the shape of its subject matter. For example, if the subject matter is love, the words in the poem might be arranged in the shape of a heart. Since visual presentation is the most important aspect of this type of poetry, the author is free to play with the size, **form,** and even colour of his or her poem.

Although this form of poetry is not that new, it is becoming increasingly popular among professional and student writers alike. Shape poems offer a fresh and interesting way of exploring something old and familiar. The immediate visual impact of the following shape poems is as important as the words themselves.

All that matters about poetry is the enjoyment of it . . . .

— Dylan Thomas

The Balloon

*by **Ryan Razzo** (student)*

```
            BALLOON
        FLIES HIGH ABOVE
       THE STREETS BELOW AS
      THE  BIRDS  ALL  AROUND
      SWOOP BY LIKE MOSQUITOES
      ON A SUMMER DAY. AT NIGHT IT
      LOOKS HIGH ABOVE AT THE STARS
      SHINING BRIGHT AND PROUD. THE
        BALLOON IS PUSHED ON BY THE
          LIGHT BREEZE. IT BIDS A
            QUICK GOOD-BYE TO
              ALL ITS NEW
                FRIENDS
                 AS IT


                        F
                        L
                        O
                        A
                          T
                          S

                            A
                            W
                              A
                                Y
```

Tie

Anonymous

IT USED TO BE
THE GUY WHO
WORE THE
TIE
BUT NOW
GIRLS BUY
TIES, NOT
JUST FOR GUYS
FOR THEMSELVES
THEY BUY TIES WITH
POLKA DOTS, TIES WITH
SPOTS, TIES WITH POP ART
TIES WITH WORDS ON
THEM, TIES WITH A
BIRTHSTONE, TIES
WITH PICTURES,
STRIPES AND
CHECKS.
TIES

November

*by **Anne Corkett***

sun
the
than
higher

Snow
and   fly
night   geese
comes   sky
down   of
into   ledge
the   yellow
last

Shape Poems

Under the Beach Umbrella

*by **John Hollander***

Straight
overhead now as white as
it ever gets and fiercer than we
can imagine the sun threatens Not with a hot
white eye but under a cupped palms dark plot to grow
to extend the field of shadow still no wider than our spread
of tented blue canvas Within this dark ring is no pain White beach
burns unbearably beyond a hot line where the edge of the noons blade

is
as
of
an
ax
To
go
by
it
so
as
to
be
in
or
at
or
on
it
is
to
be
of
it
as
we
all
are
even alas out of it within this fragile and shifting circle of shade

Jet

by *John Travers Moore*

1-2-30-48 passengers to far vistas, lost in a trail of vapor

carrying

the winds

splitting

the sky

sweeping

turning

readying

steadying

plane

the jet

silvers

Up

Niagara: Canadian Horseshoe Falls

*by **Myra Cohn Livingston***

```
in                                              spray
  my                                             wet
   ears                                           a
    a                                            face
     roaring                                      my
        in                                         in
          my                            mist
            eyes            fine
                      a

            f       c       s       p
            a       a       o       o
            l       l       u       u
            l       l       n       n
            i       i       d       d
            n       n       i       i
            g       g       n       n
                            g       g

    water   water   water   water   water   water   water   water

              and everything is white
```

WRITING FOCUS

D R A W I N G   W I T H   W O R D S

Using the following topics, or topics from your own imagination, create several shape poems.

First, list all the words and phrases related to each of your topics that you feel could be formed into a shape poem. Resources you might consult include books, magazines, billboards, labels…anything.

COMPUTER TIP

If you have access to a graphics program, you can get your poem to "flow" into the shape you want by "wrapping" the text around an outline of a shape and then "hiding" the shape.

Then, allow the position of the words and letters to act out their meaning. Apart from the words being arranged in a shape consistent with the subject matter, you are bound only by the limits of your imagination.

- touchdown
- an animal
- landmark
- shell
- eye

- gift
- love
- doorway
- frown
- heartbeat

- a fruit
- star
- a lit candle
- tree stump
- Olympics

WRITING FOCUS

LIFE AND MOTION

Work with a small group to create a shape poem that visually suggests the actions of some mammal, reptile, insect, or bird. You may want to incorporate a sense of motion in your poem in the same way that John Travers Moore did in his poem "Jet" (p. 67). If one of your group members is familiar with miming techniques, she or he may be willing to perform the movements of your chosen animal as a means of inspiration.

WRITING FOCUS

IT MAKES SENSE

Create a shape poem using words that are associated with the senses of sight and/or hearing. For example, the word "sizzle" might be written several times in a wavy pattern to suggest the subject of bacon.

FRANK & ERNEST reprinted by permission of NEA, Inc.

WRITING FOCUS

A P I C T U R E   I S   W O R T H ...

Working with a partner, choose a topic for a shape poem. Using old magazines and newspapers, cut out appropriate words and phrases related to your topic. Experiment with arranging the words in a way that illustrates your topic.

As an alternative, select a cliché or motto that you could adapt into a shape poem; for example: "kettle of fish," "can of worms," "don't cry over spilt milk," and so on.

SHARING AND PUBLISHING

Find or design an interesting background on which to display one of your shape poems. You might consider writing your poem on the actual object; for example, the poem "Tie" could be written on an old tie using fabric paint. Or, try creating a three-dimensional shape such as a mobile out of your words. Display your poem in the classroom.

Shape Poems

Photograph to Poem

a s art forms, photography and poetry may seem far apart, but they have much in common. Each tries to capture a moment in time and freeze it for the future. Photographs are excellent sources of ideas for poems because they suggest characters, settings, plots, **themes**, and **images**.

Look through your family's photograph albums. Study the faces, the clothes, the hairstyles. Are the people posing or were they interrupted in the middle of something when the photo was taken? What might they be feeling or thinking? How do you imagine their lives at the time? What multitude of ideas do these captured moments in time suggest?

All of the following poems were inspired by photographs. As you read each one, try to visualize the original image.

Ansel Adams's "Moonrise"

*by **Julie Latham** (student)*

A pale, white eye in the sky, veined
    with thick, grey patches of mist
Stares from a black, starless, void
    far above the mountains
Onto a row of dull, brown houses.

Tumbleweed litters the dry, desert
    floor like balls of crumpled paper.
Among the dead houses are bone-white
    gravestone crosses standing crookedly in
      their places
Stuck carelessly in the hard ground.
They lean sideways, forwards, and
    backwards
As gaunt as beggars.

Is there life in this place
    besides the moon's searching eye?

A town full of ghosts carries no such
    thing.

Words are things, and a small drop of ink, falling like dew upon a thought,

Photograph to Poem

72

Sixty Years

by *Jeff Wright* (student)

My family is
brown sepia,
black and white,
relatives
sitting beside their canvas tent
by the Rhine,
standing in a wild flower meadow
holding their bikes
in the Odenwald,
in a green field
in Alberta
with the new Studebaker,
drinking from large German beer glasses
at a red and white-checked table
with old Uncle Jacob and his spiralling cigar smoke,
stiffly posing,
flowers and suits,
forcing beauty,
smiles
that haven't faded
in sixty years.

produces that which makes thousands, perhaps millions think.

— **Lord Byron**

Photograph to Poem

The Car in the Picture

*by **Patricia Hampl***

My father is sitting on the grass
in a sleeveless cotton-ribbed undershirt.
He is looking off somewhere
to something we will never know about.
It must be night, it must be summer.
I am laughing. Chokecherry lips, tiny peg teeth.
My hand is touching his shoulder,
a daughter's doll hand,
hot ingot of joy impressing
itself into his life.
Behind us, that black car,
a case of beer on the running board,
a Chevy, "from before the war," as my father says.
From before me,
from the August nights when the men sat
together on the grass, watching
the green frill of the algae
lighten on the lake and become ghostly.
When someone would break
the silence to say,
You buy a Studebaker,
you buy a Rambler,
you'll never be sorry.

Photograph to Poem

Stark Boughs on the Family Tree

by **Mary Oliver**

Up in the attic row on row,
In dusty frames, with stubborn eyes,
My thin ancestors slowly fade
Under the flat Ohio skies.

And so, I think they always were:
Like their own portrait, years ago,
They paced the blue and windy fields,
Aged in the polished rooms below.

For name by name I find no sign
Of hero in this distant life,
But only men as calm as snow
Who took some faithful girl as wife,

Who labored while the drought, the flood
Crisscrossed the fickle summer air,
Who built great barns and propped their lives
Upon a slow heart-breaking care.

Why do I love them as I do,
Who dared no glory, won no fame?
In a harsh land that lies subdued,
They are the good boughs of my name.

If music sailed their dreams at all,
They were not heroes, and slept on;
As one by one they left the small
Accomplished, till the great was done.

Before Two Portraits of My Mother

*by **Émile Nelligan***
(translated by George Johnston)

I love the beautiful young girl of this
portrait, my mother, painted years ago
when her forehead was white, and there was no
shadow in the dazzling Venetian glass

of her gaze. But this other likeness shows
the deep trenches across her forehead's white
marble. The rose poem of her youth that
her marriage sang is far behind. Here is

my sadness: I compare these portraits, one
of a joy-radiant brow, the other care-
heavy: sunrise—and the thick coming on

of night. And yet how strange my ways seem,
for when I look at these faded lips my heart
smiles, but at the smiling girl my tears start.

WRITING FOCUS

MAGAZINE PHOTOGRAPHS

Search through magazines and newspapers for interesting photographs and select a photo with people in it. The photograph may be serious or humorous. For reference purposes, cut it out or arrange to have it photocopied.

Carefully examine the picture, and try to answer the following questions: *What* is happening? *Who* is doing what? *Where* and *when* is the action taking place? *How* is the picture making you feel?

Photograph to Poem

Write a rough-draft description of the picture as if you were describing it for someone who cannot see it. Give the photo a title. If the photo has more than one person in it, consider making up some dialogue. Notice facial expressions, gestures, postures. What might the individuals be feeling? Write a poem based on the photograph.

WRITING FOCUS

DIFFERENT PERSPECTIVES

Bring to class a photograph that you feel presents a unique perspective on the subject matter. In a small group, discuss what you see in each group members' photograph in as much detail as possible. Focus your attention on the people, landscapes, clothes, trees, architecture, light, and shadow.

Based on the group's discussion of your photograph, write a photo poem. You might use one of the following perspectives:

a) The poem as authored by the photographer.
b) The poem as authored by someone or something in the photograph.
c) The poem as authored by someone (or something) in the photograph who is addressing the photographer.
d) The poem as addressed to someone who has not seen the photograph.
e) The poem as addressed to someone in the photograph.
f) The poem as addressed to the photographer.

You might consider what happened just before and just after the photograph was taken. What happened as the photograph was being taken? You might also write the poem as if you found the photograph years after it was taken.

A N A L Y Z I N G   P H O T O G R A P H S

Take some of your own photographs of people (with their permission, of course). See if you can capture individuals in moments of strong emotion. Discuss the photographs in a small group, keeping in mind such aspects as the subject, format (black and white, or colour), background, emotional impact, physical point of view, **mood,** angle, and lighting.

Choose one of the photographs discussed with your small group, or a family photograph—either real or imagined—filled with many people. The occasion might be a family reunion, a wedding, a birthday celebration. Assume the role of one of the characters in the picture and think about what might be on this person's mind. Once you have formulated your character's thoughts and feelings, shape them into a photo poem.

SHARING AND PUBLISHING

Our society has many heroes. Bring to class a picture of someone who is considered by many to be a hero. In your notebook, list his or her qualities and briefly explain why you think this person is a hero. Include in your description where and when the person lived, what she or he did to become a hero, and the ways in which the heroic image of this person has been kept alive.

Share the information you discovered about your hero with a small group. Try to answer any questions your classmates may have about your hero. Then, work on your own to convert your ideas and any relevant comments contributed by your classmates into a rough draft of a **free-verse** poem. Continue to revise your poem until you are satisfied with it.

Create a class photo album that contains at least one "hero" poem and its corresponding photograph from every student.

Found Poems

It has been said that good prose *is* poetry. In actual fact, many poems begin as prose. There are, however, four characteristics of poetry that distinguish it from prose: (i) poetry tends to be more compressed, and to suggest more than prose might in the same amount of space; (ii) poetry is often more imaginative and uses more comparisons, more surprises; (iii) poetry has a more regular **rhythm** than prose does; and, (iv) poetry usually has an interesting shape or **form**.

Since prose writers often use **imagery**, figurative language, and other literary devices associated with poetry, their work can be a source of inspiration for poets. Writing poems based on different types of prose is interesting work, and the final product is known as **found poetry**.

The writer of a found poem takes words, phrases, and sentences that are discovered in public communications—such as advertisements, menus, signs, and reports—and arranges them into lines and **stanzas** to form a new and interesting perspective on the subject matter. Sources for found poems surround us every day. Sometimes a poet will rearrange the words and phrases to make his or her creation more poetic. Most poets, however, leave the original wording intact.

The following found poems were inspired by a variety of sources, from newspaper headlines to highway signs.

Our Beautiful Society

*by **Kelly Armstrong** (student)*

Babies crying,
People dying,
A Boy And His Gun...
"If you have gun power...you're growing up these days."
As harpoons fly...
The Hunt,
The Furor,
Save the Whales
GUILTY...
After a split verdict,
L.A. struggles to heal its wounds...
Teens and Sex
AIDS...
O.J.
Hitting back at terrorists
Violence,
Violence,
Violence...
What is the world coming to?

Monopoly

*by **John Robert Colombo***

GO TO JAIL
MOVE DIRECTLY TO JAIL
DO NOT PASS "GO"
DO NOT COLLECT $200.00

GET OUT OF JAIL FREE
THIS CARD MAY BE KEPT
UNTIL NEEDED OR SOLD

MAKE GENERAL REPAIRS
ON ALL OF YOUR HOUSES
FOR EACH HOUSE PAY $25.00
FOR EACH HOTEL PAY $100.00

   BANK ERROR IN YOUR FAVOUR
   COLLECT $200.00

PAY SCHOOL TAX
OF $150.00

   LIFE INSURANCE MATURES
   COLLECT $100.00

PARKING FINE
$15.00

   RECEIVE FOR SERVICES
   $25.00

YOU ARE ASSESSED
FOR STREET REPAIRS
$40.00 PER HOUSE
$115.00 PER HOTEL

   WE'RE OFF THE GOLD STANDARD
   COLLECT $50.00

PAY A $10.00 FINE
OR TAKE A "CHANCE"

   YOU HAVE WON SECOND PRIZE
   IN A BEAUTY CONTEST
   COLLECT $11.00

Of All Places!

*by **Sharon Stewart***

Ecum Secum, Bella Bella,
Bella Coola, Kleena Kleene,
Avataktoo, Abenakis,
Tuktoyaktuk, Spillimacheen.
Magpie, Owlseye,
Wildcat, Medicine Hat,
Flin Flon, Wabi-Kon
Dogpound, Owen Sound.
Minnewakan, Minnehaha,
Massawippi, Mushaboom,
Spuzzum, Snowball, South Chegoggin,
Sparkle City, Spanish Room.
Ops, Chin, Yarm, Yahk,
Elbow, Eyebrow, Chilliwack,
Bic, Bird, Love, Rose,
Jelly, Joggins, Jerrys Nose.
Buzzard, Badger, Beaver-Crossing,
Pingle, Pugwash, Pointe-au-Pic,
Dragon, Drobot, Dumpling Harbour,
Tignish, Tusket, Ta Ta Creek.
Old Crow, Ebb and Flow,
Anagance, Come-By-Chance,
Squirreltown, Blow Me Down,
Donegal, Woodpecker Hall.
CHIMNEY TICKLE!
PICKLE CROW!!
PUNKEYDOODLE'S CORNERS!!!

A Charm for Our Time

*by **Eve Merriam***

HIGHWAY   TURNPIKE   THRUWAY   MALL

DIAL DIRECT LONG DISTANCE CALL

FREEZE-DRY   HIGH-FI   PAPERBACK

JET LAG   NO SAG   VENDING SNACK

MENTHOLATED SHAVING STICK

TAPE RECORDER   CAMERA CLICK

SUPERSONIC   LIFETIME   SUB

DAYGLO   DISCOUNT   CREDIT CLUB

MOTEL   KEYCHAIN   ASTRODOME

INSTAMATIC   LOTION   FOAM

ZIPCODE   BALLPOINT

—BURN BURGER BURN!—

NO DEPOSIT

NO RETURN

Reread several of the poems in this unit and note how the writers use compression and rephrasing. When converting prose into a found poem, take into account the following:

- Write in **free-verse** form.
- Keep complete sentences together. You may use incomplete sentences, but your thoughts should be complete.
- Delete unnecessary words and adjust punctuation.
- Only use capital letters to begin a new statement or thought, not a new line.
- Indent lines for dramatic emphasis.
- Double-space between stanzas for separation of thoughts.

With these steps in mind, select an interesting and descriptive passage from a story or novel you have recently read. Arrange and rearrange the lines, phrases, and words to give the prose passage the look of a free-verse poem. Try to capture the **tone** of the prose piece in your poem. Change the sentences into various combinations of lines of poetry. Remember to divide the passage into lines which work well together and which have some kind of impact.

In a small group, discuss some of the events and key issues currently facing your community, city, province, and country. Imagine that your group has been assigned the task of creating a time capsule that will inform future generations about what life was like today. What items should be included in the capsule? Refer to magazines, food containers, labels, newspapers, and other public material for ideas.

Found Poems

Work together to make an inventory of items you would include in a capsule to be opened in 100 years. First, list as many items as you can think of. Then, negotiate among yourselves to pare the list of items down to ten or fifteen. Be prepared to defend your final choices.

From this information, write a "time capsule" found poem. Your word arrangements (typographical arrangements if you are typing) are very important. Share your time capsule poem with your classmates.

WRITING FOCUS

CANADIAN PLACE NAMES

Reread the poem "Of All Places!" on page 82. In a small group, brainstorm a list of approximately thirty to fifty unusual Canadian place names. You might want to consult two or three different atlases for ideas. Which names have their origins in Aboriginal settlement, England, Scotland, France, the Ukraine, Germany, Ireland, Italy, and so on?

> ### COMPUTER TIP
>
> If you keep your journal on a computer, you can make a found poem by reviewing your journal entries for interesting phrases, and using the "copy" and "paste" functions to copy the phrases into a new poem.

Working together and using the group-generated list of place names, write a rough draft of a found poem. You may include other words—in English or from the language of the place names—to clarify your poem. Try to make a statement about the landscape, atmosphere, or culture of Canada.

As an alternative, list all the street names you see on the way home from school. Write a found poem about your neighbourhood, incorporating the street names, along with other words appearing on retail stores, businesses, billboards, street signs, and so on.

WRITING FOCUS

M E D I A   A S   A   S O U R C E

Use a brief passage of text from a magazine or newspaper article as a source for words, phrases, and sentences that may be collected into a poem. Select a topic that has special meaning for you and write a found poem using lines and parts of lines from your source text. Design a creative way in which to display your poem and the source text together.

SHARING AND PUBLISHING

Magazine

You might consider compiling a class "magazine" of found poems bound by a front and back cover. Consider using a collage of "found" objects to illustrate your cover.

Time Capsule

Create an actual time capsule based on your poem and obtain permission to bury it somewhere on school grounds. Be sure to include a copy of your poem in the time capsule. Invite the yearbook committee or school newspaper to cover the event.

. . . the poem means more, not less than ordinary speech can communicate.

— T.S. Eliot

Ballads

he **ballad** is one of the oldest forms of poetry and has its roots in storytelling traditions. Ballads are **narrative poems** which are either sung or recited. During the Middle Ages, singing poets called "minstrels" or "troubadours," wandered throughout Europe performing ballads in castles and villages. Because traditional ballads were preserved by word of mouth from generation to generation, and the original authors were usually unknown, different versions (both text and tune) of the same ballad may exist. Today, the word "ballad" refers to these traditional poems and also to more modern songs and narrative poems which share similar characteristics of subject matter, **form**, **rhythm**, and **rhyme**.

Ballads are often written about legendary people or historical events—Robin Hood was one of the most popular subjects of early English ballads—but a ballad may also describe an adventure, a love story, a domestic tragedy, the supernatural, or an incident from everyday life. The storyline or plot is usually condensed in a ballad and is conveyed using dialogue. In many ballads, the same lines are repeated throughout, with a bit of information added each time. In addition, ballads often contain a **refrain**.

Rhythm and rhyme are two key elements in ballads. Traditional ballads are typically organized in four-line **stanzas** called **quatrains**. Each quatrain has a regular rhythm with alternating four-stress and three-stress lines; the second and fourth lines of each quatrain generally rhyme. This regular rhythm and rhyme, along with the informal **diction**, make ballads easy to remember.

As the following four "modern" samples illustrate, the ballad is still a popular poetic form.

A Sailor's Love

by **Erin Claussen** (student)

The roaring surf crashed o'er the rocks,
A sad, young maid stood lonely,
Waiting for her brave young sailor,
He was her one and only.

She'd waited long, through many nights,
That he should come back to her.
He'd promised that he would return,
When last he'd come to woo her.

Then through the mist he came in sight,
His step was light and eerie,
His hair was white, no longer dark,
His face was gaunt and weary.

She wondered how he had come,
There was no ship in sight.
It struck her he was different,
She turned from him in fright.

"Don't turn from me my precious love,"
Up from the shore she heard:
"I promised you I would return;
You see, I've kept my word."

"But why are you so pale, my dear,
Why is your face so thin?
I can see right through you,
When the moon shines on your skin."

"I've come back from the dead, my dear,
To take you by my side.
I've come for you these many miles
To take you for my bride."

And then he looked into her eyes
And turned and walked away,
And she as if now hypnotized,
Followed him into the bay.

The Cremation of Sam McGee

by **Robert Service**

There are strange things done in the midnight sun
    By the men who moil for gold;
The Arctic trails have their secret tales
    That would make your blood run cold;
The Northern Lights have seen queer sights,
    But the queerest they ever did see
Was that night on the marge of Lake Lebarge
    I cremated Sam McGee.

Now Sam McGee was from Tennessee,
     where the cotton blooms and blows.
Why he left his home in the South to roam
     round the Pole, God only knows.
He was always cold, but the land of gold seemed
     to hold him like a spell;
Though he'd often say in his homely way that
     "he'd sooner live in hell."

On a Christmas Day we were mushing our way
     over the Dawson Trail.
Talk of your cold! Through the parka's fold it stabbed
     like a driven nail.
If our eyes we'd close, then the lashes froze
     till sometimes we couldn't see;
It wasn't much fun, but the only one to whimper
     was Sam McGee.

And that very night, as we lay packed tight
     in our robes beneath the snow,
And the dogs were fed, and the stars o'erhead
     were dancing heel and toe,
He turned to me, and "Cap," says he, "I'll cash in
     this trip, I guess;
And if I do, I'm asking that you won't refuse
     my last request."

Well, he seemed so low that I couldn't say no;
     then he says with a sort of moan:
"It's the cursèd cold, and it's got right hold till I'm
     chilled clean through to the bone.
Yet 'tain't being dead—it's my awful dread of the
     icy grave that pains;
So I want you to swear that, foul or fair, you'll
     cremate my last remains."

A pal's last need is a thing to heed, so I swore
    I would not fail;
And we started on at the streak of dawn; but God!
    He looked ghastly pale.
He crouched on the sleigh, and he raved all day
    of his home in Tennessee;
And before nightfall a corpse was all that was left
    of Sam McGee.

There wasn't a breath in that land of death, and I
    hurried, horror-driven,
With a corpse half hid that I couldn't get rid,
    because of a promise given;
It was lashed to the sleigh, and it seemed to say:
    "You may tax your brawn and brains,
But you promised true, and it's up to you to cremate
    those last remains."

Now a promise made is a debt unpaid, and the trail
    has its own stern code.
In the days to come, though my lips were dumb,
    in my heart how I cursed that load.
In the long, long night, by the lone firelight,
    while the huskies, round in a ring,
Howled out their woes to the homeless snows—
    O God! How I loathed the thing.

And every day that quiet clay seemed to heavy
    and heavier grow;
And on I went, though the dogs were spent and the
    grub was getting low;
The trail was bad, and I felt half mad, but I swore
    I would not give in;
And I'd often sing to the hateful thing, and it
    harkened with a grin.

Till I came to the marge of Lake Lebarge, and a
        derelict there lay;
It was jammed in the ice, but I saw in a trice
        it was called the *Alice May*.
And I looked at it, and I thought a bit, and I looked
        at my frozen chum;
Then "Here," said I, with a sudden cry,
        "is my cre-ma-tor-eum."

Some planks I tore from the cabin floor, and I lit
        the boiler fire;
Some coal I found that was lying around,
        and I heaped the fuel higher;
The flames just soared, and the furnace roared—such
        a blaze you seldom see;
And I burrowed a hole in the flowing coal, and
        I stuffed in Sam McGee.

Then I made a hike, for I didn't like to hear
        him sizzle so;
And the heavens scowled, and the huskies howled,
        and the wind began to blow.
It was icy cold, but the hot sweat rolled down my
        cheeks, and I don't know why;
And the greasy smoke in an inky cloak went
        streaking down the sky.

I do not know how long in the snow I wrestled
        with grisly fear;
But the stars came out and they danced about
        ere again I ventured near;
I was sick with dread, but I bravely said:
        "I'll just take a peep inside.
I guess he's cooked, and it's time I looked;"
        …then the door I opened wide.

And there sat Sam, looking cool and calm,
    and in the heart of the furnace roar;
And he wore a smile you could see a mile, and he
    said: "Please close that door.
It's fine in here, but I greatly fear you'll let in
    the cold and storm!
Since I left Plumtree, down in Tennessee, it's the first
    time I've been warm."

There are strange things done in the midnight sun
    By the men who moil for gold;
The Arctic trails have their secret tales
    That would make your blood run cold;
The Northern Lights have seen queer sights,
    But the queerest they ever did see
Was that night on the marge of Lake Lebarge
    I cremated Sam McGee.

Claude Dallas

*by **Ian Tyson and Tom Russell***

In a land the Spanish once had called
  the Northern Mystery
Where the rivers run and disappear
And the Mustang still lives free
By the Devil's wash and the coyote
  hole
In the wild Owyee Range
Somewhere in the sage tonight
The wind calls out his name
Aye Aye Aye

Come gather round me buckaroos
And the story I will tell
The fugitive Claude Dallas

Who just broke out of jail
You might think this tale is history
From before the West was won
But the events that I'll describe took
  place in 1981

He was born out in Virginia
Left home when school was through
In the deserts of Nevada
He became a buckaroo
He learned the ways of cattle
He learned to sit a horse
He always packed a pistol
And he practised deadly force

Then Claude he became a trapper
He dreamed of the bygone days
He studied bobcat logic
In the wild and silent ways
In the bloody runs near paradise
In the monitors down south
Trapping cats and coyotes
Living hand and mouth
Aye Aye Aye

Then Claude took to living all alone
Out many miles from town
A friend Jim Stevens brought supplies
And he stayed to hang around
That day two wardens Pogue and Elms
Drove in to check Claude out
They were seeking violations
And to see what Claude's about

Now Claude had hung some venison
Had a bobcat pelt or two
Pogue claimed they were out of season
He says, "Dallas, you're all through"
But Dallas would not leave his camp
He refused to go to town
As the wind howled through the bull
    camp
They stared each other down

It's hard to say what happened next
Perhaps we'll never know
They were going to take Claude into jail
And he'd vowed he'd never go
Jim Stevens heard the gunfire

And when he turned around
Bill Pogue was fallin' backwards
Conley Elms he fell face down
Aye Aye Aye

Jim Stevens walked on over
There was a gun near Bill Pogue's hand
It's hard to say who'd drawn his first
But Claude had made his stand
Claude said, "I'm justified Jim…
They were going to cut me down…
A man's got a right to hang some meat
When he's livin' this far from town."

It took 18 men and 15 months
To finally run Claude down
In the sage outside of paradise
They drove him to the ground
Convicted up in Idaho
Manslaughter by decree
Thirty years at maximum
But soon Claude would break free

There's two sides to this story
There may be no right or wrong
The lawman and the renegade
Have graced a thousand songs
So the story is an old one
Conclusion's hard to draw
But Claude's out in the sage tonight
He may be the last outlaw
Aye Aye Aye

Repeat 1st Verse

Mulga Bill's Bicycle

*by **A.B. Paterson***

'Twas Mulga Bill, from Eaglehawk, that caught the cycling craze;
He turned away the good old horse that served him many days;
He dressed himself in cycling clothes, resplendent to be seen;
He hurried off to town and bought a shining new machine;
And as he wheeled it through the door, with air of lordly pride.
The grinning shop assistant said, "Excuse me, can you ride?"

"See, here, young man," said Mulga Bill, "from Walgett to the sea,
From Conroy's Gap to Castlereagh, there's none can ride like me.
I'm good all round at everything, as everybody knows,
Although I'm not the one to talk—I *hate* a man that blows.
But riding is my special gift, my chiefest, sole delight;
Just ask a wild duck can it swim, a wild cat can it fight.
There's nothing walks or jumps or runs, on axle, hoof, or wheel,
But what I'll sit, while hide will hold and girths and straps are tight:
I'll ride this here two-wheeled concern right straight away at sight."

'Twas Mulga Bill, from Eaglehawk, that sought his own abode,
That perched above the Dead Man's Creek, beside the mountain road.
He turned the cycle down the hill and mounted for the fray,
But ere he'd gone a dozen yards it bolted clean away.
It left the track, and through the trees, just like a silver streak,
It whistled down the awful slope, towards the Dead Man's Creek.
It shaved a stump by half an inch, it dodged a big white-box:
The very wallaroos in fright went scrambling up the rocks,
The wombats hiding in their caves dug deeper underground,
As Mulga Bill, as white as chalk, sat tight to every bound.
It struck a stone and gave a spring that cleared a fallen tree,
It raced beside a precipice as close as close could be;
And then as Mulga Bill let out one last despairing shriek
It made a leap of twenty feet into the Dead Man's Creek.

'Twas Mulga Bill, from Eaglehawk, that slowly swam ashore:
He said, "I've had some narrer shaves and lively rides before;
I've rode a wild bull round a yard to win a five-pound bet,
But this was the most awful ride that I've encountered yet.
I'll give that two-wheeled outlaw best; it's shaken all me nerve
To feel it whistle through the air and plunge and buck and swerve.
It's safe at rest in Dead Man's Creek, we'll leave it lying still:
A horse's back is good enough henceforth for Mulga Bill."

WRITING FOCUS

HISTORICAL BALLAD

See if you can write one or two ballad stanzas (or indeed an entire ballad!) on one of the following topics:

- the historical origin of a Canadian city
- a famous Canadian event or tragedy such as a sea or mining disaster
- an experience from the point of view of an early Canadian hunter, fisher, teacher, lumberjack, homesteader, explorer, military leader, or politician
- a historical topic of your choice

WRITING FOCUS

ALL-CANADIAN BALLAD

There are hundreds of words which are native to Canada and which are found in Canadian ballads. Write a short ballad using some of the following "Canadianisms," or some that you find yourself. As the subject for your ballad, you might consider a situation involving a scary incident, an encounter with a rival, an accident, or an unexpected arrival. Ensure your ballad tells a brief, dramatic story in simple language. Your ballad may be written in **couplets** or without **rhyme**.

aglu – a breathing-hole in ice, made by seals

badlands – an arid region in southern Alberta characterized by severe erosion and strange land formations, and containing dinosaur and other fossils

crowbar palace – slang for "a jail"

dance hall – a building used for public dancing

egg-beater – very small outboard motor

fiddler's elbow – a sharp turn in a road

gold rush – a vast movement of persons to a new goldfield

high muckamuck – (slang) a leading person in a group; big-shot

iron horse – a railway locomotive

johnnycake – a thin, flat cake made of cornmeal

King's Pine – choice white pine marked with a broad arrow and claimed as government property for use as spars and masts for the Navy (policy pursued in Nova Scotia)

logging bee – a gathering of neighbours to clear land by logging

COMPUTER TIP

When you are ready to submit your poems to your teacher for evaluation, try using the "spell check" feature to double check your work. Remember, however, that a computerized spell check will not recognize all errors. Proofread carefully.

SHARING AND PUBLISHING

Write your name and a possible first line to a ballad on a blank piece of paper. Ensure that the last three words appear on a separate line. Fold the paper so that only these three words are showing and pass your paper to the student next to you. When you receive another student's paper, write the next line to the ballad based on the three words you can see. Allow three or so minutes before folding the paper and passing it to the next student. Continue this process until each student's paper has been filled. Read your collaboratively written ballad aloud to the class.

Parodies

many poems duplicate the **rhythm** pattern and/or **rhyme** scheme of popular, well-known poems. These "copycat" poems are called parodies.

Parodies are usually written for their humorous effect. Often the writer of the **parody** (the "parodist") exaggerates certain aspects of the original writer's style. To be able to do this, of course, she or he must have a feel for the original poem and the techniques used by the writer.

Some poems naturally lend themselves to parody better than others. The poetry of William Carlos Williams, for example, is frequently parodied because Williams tends to use very few words to convey a simple message. Notice the precision and clarity of language in "This Is Just To Say," which follows.

Imitation is the sincerest [form] of flattery.

— Charles Caleb Colton

▶ This Is Just To Say

by *William Carlos Williams*

I have eaten
the plums
that were in
the icebox

and which
you were probably
saving
for breakfast

Forgive me
they were delicious
so sweet
and so cold

Williams' poetry reveals the concrete **images** of our daily lives and makes us keenly aware of the richness of those images. Read the two student parodies of "This Is Just To Say" on page 99. Notice how the simple realities of life are handled by the authors.

PEANUTS reprinted by permission of UFS, Inc.

This Is Just To Say

(With apologies to W.C.W.) by **Kristie Hodges** *(student)*

I have read your
diary
that was in
your dresser drawer,

and which
you were probably
hiding
from me.

Forgive me,
sister,
I couldn't help myself…
I was curious
to find out
about
your wonderful life.

This Is Just To Say

("Forgive me, William Carlos Williams") by **Allan Harms** *(student)*

I have reset
your clock,
so you were late
for school,

you were
called down
to the office…
and got grounded.

Forgive me,
but it was so tempting,
in fact—
so irresistible!

Parodies

Another type of poem that is often parodied is the action poem. Notice which images student author Michael Janzen chose to spoof in "Smash Time," his parody of Edwin A. Hoey's "Foul Shot."

▶ Foul Shot

*by **Edwin A. Hoey***

With two 60's stuck on the scoreboard
And two seconds hanging on the clock,
The solemn boy in the center of eyes,
Squeezed by silence,
Seeks out the line with his feet,
Soothes his hands along his uniform,
Gently drums the ball against the floor,
Then measures the waiting net,
Raises the ball on his right hand,
Balances it with his left,
Calms it with fingertips,
Breathes,
Crouches,
Waits,
And then through a stretching of stillness,
Nudges it upward.

The ball
Slides up and out,
Lands,
Leans,
Wobbles,
Wavers,
Hesitates,
Exasperates,
Plays it coy
Until every face begs with unsounding screams—

And then
        And then
                And then
Right before ROAR-UP,
Dives down and through.

Smash Time

(With apologies to Edwin A. Hoey)   by ***Michael Janzen*** *(student)*

With one more point to go
And the score is tied,
The birdie goes up over the net
towards me.
I take my stance,
muscles tense,
and get ready.
I swing my racket back,
the birdie makes contact.
The birdie
jumps,
soars,
curves,
flies,
Until every eye is on the white, rubber birdie.
And then

       And then,

Down

    sweeps

       the

          birdie

            and

            dives

            towards

            the

    f l o o r.

John Masefield's poem "Sea-Fever," is a well-known poem that is rich in rhythm and in **imagery.** Michelle Maddock, in her poem "Milk Fever," has duplicated that rhythm and imagery in her humorous lament about the responsibilities that come with living on a farm.

Sea-Fever

by *John Masefield*

I must go down to the seas again, to the lonely sea and the sky,
And all I ask is a tall ship and a star to steer her by,
And the wheel's kick and the wind's song and the white sail's shaking,
And a gray mist on the sea's face and a gray dawn breaking.

I must go down to the seas again, for the call of the running tide
Is a wild call and a clear call that may not be denied;
And all I ask is a windy day with the white clouds flying,
And the flung spray and the blown spume, and the sea gulls crying.

I must go down to the seas again, to the vagrant gypsy life,
To the gull's way and the whale's way where the wind's like a whetted knife;
And all I ask is a merry yarn from a laughing fellow rover,
And quiet sleep and a sweet dream when the long trick's over.

Milk Fever

(With apologies to John Masefield)

by *Michelle Maddock* (student)

I must go out to do chores again
to the lonely barn and the cows,
And all I ask is a little path
Or maybe a small snow plow,
And the cow's kick, and the cow's moo
and the cow's tail shaking,
And the cold wind on my cold face
and the grey dawn's breaking.

I must go down to do chores again
And my father yells that I'm late.
It's a wild yell and a clear yell
that seals me in my fate
And all I ask is to stay inside
and escape this daily chore.
And a warm bed to sleep in
an extra hour more.

PARODIES IN THE MEDIA

Parodies mock, "spoof," or make fun of something else. As a group, discuss any parodies that you have seen on television or at the movies. Was the exaggeration and imitation funny? What contributed to the humour?

Choose a television program or movie that your group feels would be fun to parody. Work together to outline how this program or film could be parodied, then write a poem based on your outline.

WRITING FOCUS

WITH APOLOGIES TO ...

Work through one of the following two activities.

a) Write a parody of either "Foul Shot" or "This Is Just To Say." Or, as an alternative, write a poem that parodies the codes of conduct governing your school, such as: rules about smoking/not smoking; consequences of parking in a teacher's spot; rules governing absentee notes; dress codes.

b) Reread "Sea-Fever" and "Milk Fever" on page 102. Use both poems as a "take-off" point for a parody of your own. You might begin with one of the following lines:

- "I must go down to the mall again, to the crowded shops and stores"
- "I must go off with my folks again, to relatives galore"
- "I must go down to the office again, for passing notes in class"

Consult with several classmates to ensure the rhythm pattern and rhyme scheme of your poem duplicates "Sea-Fever."

Parodies

Working with a partner, select a poem that you feel paints a clear image that could be mimicked. You might choose a poem from this anthology. Work together to write a parody of your chosen poem. Try to copy the **form** while deviating from the content as much as possible.

Or, as an alternative, imitate the style of a well-known poet. Read or listen to several samples of his or her work. Concentrate on the poet's style, voice, **diction**, **cadence**, point of view, and so on. Make sure that it is possible to identify the poet you are parodying

SHARING AND PUBLISHING

Work with a group of three or four students to create a brief skit based on your best parody poem. Once you have perfected your performance, share it with the rest of the class.

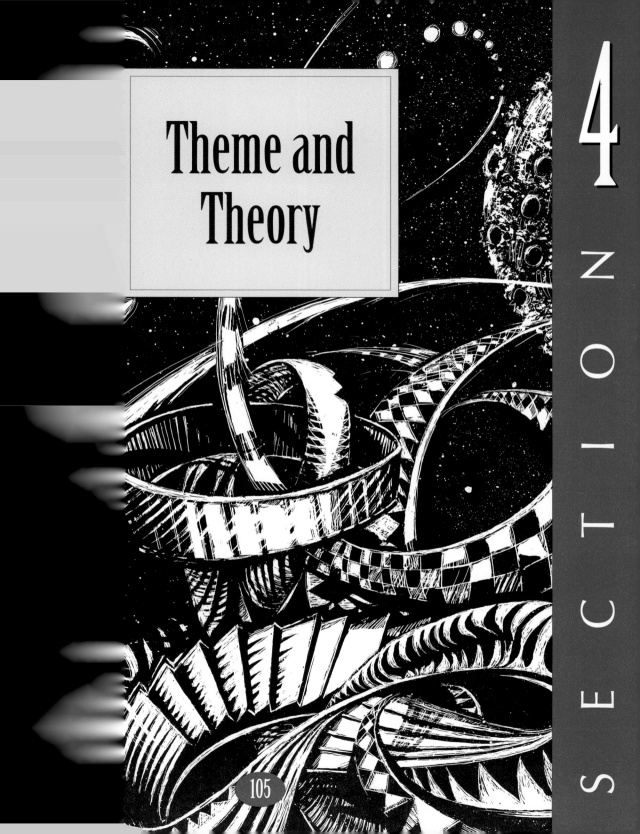

Theme and
Theory

Looking In

human beings, by nature, tend to be intrigued by their own identity and environment. At various stages in life we may ask ourselves questions such as, "Who am I?" and "How do I fit into my world?"

To answer the question, "Who am I?" you must first look within, at those characteristics which are uniquely your own. What distinguishes you from those around you? Consider your interests and feelings, your abilities, talents, and weaknesses, how you relate to other people, and how you react to different experiences.

Through this process of self-examination, you may discover strong feelings that not only influence the way you think about yourself and others, but that affect the way you behave. Understanding your feelings is part of the process in shaping your identity. It is normal and natural for people of all ages to experience a wide range of feelings such as anger, embarrassment, happiness, jealousy, sympathy, and so on. Feelings are just one characteristic of human beings that distinguish us from other life forms and help to shape our personal identities.

Often, people will use writing as a means of working through their feelings and questions of identity. One of the most popular forms of personal expression is autobiographical writing. Writing an autobiographical poem will encourage you to access memories, feelings, and beliefs that you may have hidden in your subconscious. By exploring your personal thoughts, you will find answers to the question, "Who am I?"

THE BORN LOSER® by Art and Chip Sansom

BORN LOSER reprinted by permission of NEA, Inc.

▶ Reflection

*by **Jodie Arey** (student)*

When I look
into the mirror
I sometimes wish
I could really see
myself
and know
who I am
what I want
why I do
the things I do.
Instead I see
a girl looking back
who's just as puzzled as I am.

I want, by understanding myself, to understand others.

— Katherine Mansfield

Mortality

by **Tina Carlson** (student)

I am…
I am a teenager who is scared.
I wonder where my life is going…
I see people every day who are happy
And I try to be.
I want to be happy—very much!
I am a teenager who is scared.

I pretend to be happy—as hard as it is,
I feel good when I see my Mom smile.
It helps make me smile too.
I worry about her…
But together we can get through it.
I cry when my Mom cries too.
I am a teenager who is scared.

It's over and
Life goes on…good…although
I try to think happiness.
And sometimes that works.
I dream about heaven and smile the whole time
And sometimes that works.
I hope it is as great as I dream.
I am a teenager who is scared.

Looking In

Hidden Beauty

*by **Heidi Ann Davidson** (student)*

Look past my face,
Look beyond my eyes,
For they're just a mask,
Only a disguise,
Look to the person who lives within.

Do you know my morals, my values, my sins?
Do you know my hopes, my loves and my dreams?
For I'm a more complicated person
Than I may seem.
Do you know the secrets
I feel I must hide?
Those feelings I keep bottled inside?

Have you discovered the real me?
Have you found my hidden beauty?
It's there if you search
In the right place,
But first you must learn
To look past my face…

I am invisible, understand, simply because people refuse to see me.

— Ralph Ellison

Definition

by **Matt Faulkner** (student)

You tell me I'm not an artist,
Until I've been exhibited.
You tell me I'm not a poet,
Until I've been published.

And I tell you you're not a person,
Until you've lived.
And you haven't lived,
Until you've loved,
And you haven't loved,
Until you're a poet.
(And you can love,
Without being published)

Who Am I?

by **Felice Holman**

The trees ask me,
And the sky,
And the sea asks me
    Who am I?

The grass asks me,
And the sand,
And the rocks ask me
    Who am I?

The wind tells me
At nightfall,
And the rain tells me
    Someone small.

Someone small
Someone small
    But a piece
        of
        it
        all.

Looking In

111

Reversible

by **Octavio Paz**
(translated by Eliot Weinberger)

In space
       I am
inside of me
           the space
outside of me
           the space

nowhere
       I am
outside of me
           in space

inside
      is space
outside of it
         nowhere

I am
    in space
etcetera

*Touched by poetry, language is more
fully language and at the same time is
no longer language: it is a poem.*

— Octavio Paz

Looking In

112

Hero

by *Mariah Carey*

There's a hero
If you look inside your heart
You don't have to be afraid
Of what you are
There's an answer
If you reach into your soul
And the sorrow that you know
Will melt away

And then a hero comes along
With the strength to carry on
And you cast your fears aside
And you know you can survive
So when you feel like hope is gone
Look inside you and be strong
And you'll finally see the truth
That a hero lies in you

It's a long road
When you face the world alone
No one reaches out a hand
For you to hold
You can find love
If you search within yourself
And the emptiness you felt
Will disappear

And then a hero comes along
With the strength to carry on
And you cast your fears aside
And you know you can survive
So when you feel like hope is gone
Look inside you and be strong
And you'll finally see the truth
That a hero lies in you

Lord knows
Dreams are hard to follow
But don't let anyone
Tear them away
Hold on
There will be tomorrow
In time
You'll find the way

And then a hero comes along
With the strength to carry on
And you cast your fears aside
And you know you can survive
So when you feel like hope is gone
Look inside you and be strong
And you'll finally see the truth
That a hero lies in you

Looking In

Write down some personal information about yourself such as: name, nickname, age, birthdate, place of birth, description of your birthplace, family members, trips taken, sports played, hobbies, club membership(s), particular interests, and ambitions for the future. Then, move beyond concrete details and describe yourself in terms of someone who loves, hates, envies, feels, and so on.

> ### COMPUTER TIP
>
> *If you are unhappy with the first draft of a poem, don't delete it right away. Instead, start a new page. As you write, you may find new ways to incorporate words or phrases from your first draft into your revised poem.*

Based on your personal description, develop an outline that summarizes what you would like others to know about you. Consider the way you want to be viewed by others in your outline. Write a rough draft of a **free-verse** poem titled "Me," then revise and prepare a final draft of your personal profile.

WRITING FOCUS

T H E   I N T E R V I E W

Select six or eight of the following interview-type questions. Find a partner and take turns asking each other your list of questions. You may "pass" on a question that makes you uncomfortable as long as you allow your partner to ask you a different question from the list. Record each other's responses.

a) What is your favourite colour?

b) What is your greatest talent?

c) Identify something you cannot do well.

d) What plant or animal are you most like?

e) What is your favourite food?

f) What career do you plan to pursue?

g) Name a public figure you admire.

h) What do people most often tease you about?

i) What is your favourite musical instrument?

j) What is your pet peeve?

k) Compare the colour of your eyes, hair, and skin with something else.

l) With what appliance or object might you compare yourself?

m) What is your favourite sport?

n) What do you most fear?

o) Do you have any unique mannerisms?

p) What is your strongest character trait?

q) What specific words might be used to describe your walk?

r) Create a new nickname for yourself.

Exchange notes with your partner. Distill some of the more interesting points and information she or he gleaned from you during the interview into a poem about yourself. Then, work with your partner to edit your poem in light of the following questions:

- Are the lines divided in the best places?
- Does the positioning of the lines create an interesting **rhythm?**
- Are the figures of speech fresh and accurate?
- Does the poem appeal to the senses?
- Is the spelling correct?
- Does the poem accurately reflect the information revealed during the interview?

Poetry is the profession of private truth, supported by craftsmanship in the use of words ....

— Robert Graves

Personalized Souvenir

Obtain or create a two-sided (either front and back, or side by side) portfolio suitable for display. On one side, attach a recent picture of yourself. On the other side, attach your best autobiographical poem that you wrote during the course of this unit. Choose a trusted friend or family member to whom you would feel comfortable giving this intimate souvenir of yourself.

Yearbook Caption

Work with a small group and, based on one of your autobiographical poems, write an appropriate caption that might appear under your school yearbook picture. Ensure everyone has a copy of his or her group-written caption. The captions can be as funny or as serious as you and/or the group members wish.

Family Times

The family is perhaps the oldest of humankind's social institutions, existing long before any government or religious organization. Families are found in the simplest of human societies, and among the animal kingdom as well. In every part of the world, from primitive times to the present, humans have tried to satisfy their deepest needs for love, acceptance, moral support, and so on, through their family relationships. Although families exist in many different forms (the traditional nuclear family, the single family, the foster family, the extended family), one of the great and enduring benefits of family life is the sense of "connectedness" it provides from generation to generation.

The following list outlines some trends regarding the Canadian family that are emerging during this last decade of the twentieth century:

- With fewer children being born, the size of the family is decreasing.
- One-parent families are on the increase.
- First-time marriage rates have declined somewhat.
- The remarriage rate is rising annually.
- The poverty rate is not improving.
- Family violence, including child abuse, is increasing.

The institution of family will probably always exist in some form or another because, as the following poems show, our relationship with family members, and our place within the family unit, has a profound influence on our lives.

▶ Mother's Arms

*by **Erin Baade** (student)*

The firemen came to school
with videos of children
trapped in flames,
their mothers below
shivering in breezy nightgowns,
sobbing for their slippered feet
planted firmly on the cold ground.

My bedroom in grade one
was on the second floor,
far too high to jump.
Every night out my window
I saw you, Mom,
standing beneath me
in your blue flannel
housecoat, the family
album clutched to your chest,
eyes reflecting
my burning walls,
until you came
to say goodnight
and I slept,
your arms wrapped around me
like a fire blanket.

The Photo

*by **Tara Holmes** (student)*

A girl
I once knew as my sister
hair long as a fitted shirt
lake brown eyes,
alive with the moonlight
falling on her baby moon face,
sat on the veranda
last night
and I reminded her
of the days when
we were like clouds
in a thunder storm
fighting for attention,
those cling-on days,
the two of us growths
hanging from our mother's legs,
and how once
when we sat on the swing
my father
got out his new camera and
the ruffles on our dresses
waved like the days going by
our smiles still competing
in that one picture
Dad took.

Those Winter Sundays

*by **Robert Hayden***

Sundays too my father got up early
and put his clothes on in the blueblack cold,
then with cracked hands that ached
from labor in the weekday weather made
banked fires blaze. No one ever thanked him.

I'd wake and hear the cold splintering, breaking.
When the rooms were warm, he'd call,
and slowly I would rise and dress,
fearing the chronic angers of that house,

Speaking indifferently to him,
who had driven out the cold
and polished my good shoes as well.
What did I know, what did I know
of love's austere and lonely offices?

Grandmother

i remember your hands
making placinta in the Old House
in the sunny kitchen, your hands
strong and warm, shape the batter
on an old wood table scrubbed clean

thinner & thinner, your hands
stretch and pull the batter
thin as paper, thin as onion skins
a thousand times i thought
the skin would tear   you laughed &
held it to the light
the light showed through &
the shape of your face

your hands were brown & strong
but soft   my own young hands
seemed rough when i touched yours
your hands never hesitated, wondering
how much? they reached and scooped
handfuls of raisins and brown sugar
never hesitated, wondering
how is this done? will it tear?
am i doing it right?

my hands have other skills
i place them on the typewriter
and make the keys fly
even with my eyes closed

Birdfoot's Grampa

*by **Joseph Bruchac III***

The old man
must have stopped our car
two dozen times to climb out
and gather into his hands
the small toads blinded
by our lights and leaping,
live drops of rain.

The rain was falling,
a mist about his white hair
and I kept saying
you can't save them all,
accept it, get back in
we've got places to go.

But, leathery hands full
of wet brown life,
knee deep in the summer
roadside grass,
he just smiled and said
they have places to go to
too.

*I could not have slept tonight if
I had left that helpless little creature
to perish on the ground.*

— Abraham Lincoln
*Lincoln's reply to friends who
chided him for delaying them
by stopping to return a fledgling
to her nest.*

Family Times

Mid-Term Break

*by **Seamus Heaney***

I sat all morning in the college sick bay
Counting bells knelling classes to a close.
At two o'clock our neighbours drove me home.

In the porch I met my father crying —
He had always taken funerals in his stride —
And Big Jim Evans saying it was a hard blow.

The baby cooed and laughed and rocked the pram
When I came in, and I was embarrassed
By old men standing up to shake my hand

And tell me they were 'sorry for my trouble';
Whispers informed strangers I was the eldest,
Away at school, as my mother held my hand

In hers and coughed out angry tearless sighs.
At ten o'clock the ambulance arrived
With the corpse, stanched and bandaged by the nurses.

Next morning I went up into the room. Snowdrops
And candles soothed the bedside; I saw him
For the first time in six weeks. Paler now.

Wearing a poppy bruise on his left temple,
He lay in the four foot box as in his cot.
No gaudy scars, the bumper knocked him clear.

A four foot box, a foot for every year.

Precious Bits of Family

by **Linda Belarde**

Some memories stand out
sitting in the kitchen
canning fish smoked in our smokehouse
with Mom, Aunt, sisters, cousins
Listening to the news of the first moon landing
Telling Gramma that yes, there're men on the moon
but we can't see them.
She looks puzzled
as if we are crazy
but listens politely
as nice people often do to crazies.
The berry-picking trips
dreaded because everyone else was on a picnic
turning into our own picnic
with crackers and soda pop and blueberries
and laughter over who ate more than they picked.

In my own very self,
I am part of my family.

— **David Herbert Lawrence**

All

by **Leona Gom**

all he would have to say is,
remember the time I came home
with a beard and Dad didn't know me,
and we would all laugh,
Mom would say, just by your voice,
I knew your voice, and my sister
would say, the dog kept barking, and
I would say, that was the
summer I got a camera.
it pulls around us
like a drawstring, that time,
when we come together,
awkward and older,
our frayed conversations
trying to thread some memory
of each other,
one of us will only have to say,
remember the time you came home
from the bush with your beard,
and we were all easy again
with each other,
someone will say how
Mom knew his voice, someone
will remember how the dog barked, I
will remember my new camera,
and we are a family again,
young and laughing
on the front porch.

Family: The we of me.
— **Carson McCullers**

A COMPARISON

Imagine an object or scene that interests you and make a mental note of its various characteristics. Use this object or scene as a **metaphor** to describe one of your parents or guardians in poetic form. Revise your poem using the questions below as a guideline:

- In what ways does my poem convey an interesting or powerful statement about the topic? How can I make it more effective?
- What, if any, words or phrases should be changed or omitted to make the poem more concise?
- How should the line arrangements be altered to place more emphasis on certain words?

WRITING FOCUS

A FICTIONAL FAMILY

With a small group, discuss several television families. How are some of these fictional family relationships presented? Do any of the families resemble your group members' families in terms of problems they face, ways they communicate with one another, lifestyle, expectations, and so on?

Choose one television family and list characteristics of the family members' relationships. Then, use your list to write a poem about your television family. Elect a group member to read your poem to the class and invite the class to guess which television show your poem is based on.

Choose one of the following activities:

a) In the poem "Mother's Arms," the author identifies one object that she imagines her mother is clutching. What is that object? Why might the mother have chosen to hold on to that object over another?

   Write a poem about one of your most treasured family mementos.

b) Reread the poems in this unit that focus on the poets' memories of one particular family member.

   Think about a memory, either good or bad, that you have of one of your family members. Write a **free-verse** poem about your relationship with this person and why the memory is so significant. Try to make the title of your poem convey your feelings about this person.

c) Work with a partner to research and write a poem about a well-known family in Canadian history, such as the Dionnes, the Donnellys, and so on. Ask your Social Studies teacher and/or the librarian to help you find appropriate resources to consult. If possible, include a photograph of the family with your poem.

SHARING AND PUBLISHING

After having written a poem or two about some aspects of life within your family, take your poems home to share with members of your family. Remember, it is easy to share your work with people you trust. By sharing your poem, you are letting others know what you believe and how you feel. Try to get into the habit of sharing your creative writing and your journal entries with trusted family members and friends.

Home Base

Where you live and the structure you call "home" plays a very important role in your life. Perhaps this is no more true than when you long to leave home, or when you have been away for a period of time and long to return.

Not only does your home shelter you from the weather and provide a place for eating, sleeping, and storing your belongings, but it is a place where most of the significant people in your life live. For this reason, where you live may be either an anchor in your life, a refuge from the sometimes harsh realities of the outside world, or it may be a place of turmoil and misery.

As the following poems suggest, people are seldom indifferent toward the place where they live or have lived. "Home" means different things to different people: comfort, peacefulness, contentment, patriotism, a sense of community, family. What does "home" mean to you?

Home is the place where, when you have to go there, they have to take you in.

— **Robert Frost**

My City

*by **Kerra Hodges** (student)*

A quiet place,
a happy place,
a do-nothing-sit-around-and-veg place.

A simple place,
a friendly place,
a million-different-fast-food-restaurants place.

A creative place,
a "country" place,
an on-your-way-to-Jasper-stop place.

A different place,
an active place,
a soccer-all-summer-long place.

A familiar place,
a comforting place…

It's my place—
Spruce Grove.

The Old House

by **Lisa Watson** (student)

In the autumn sunlight
the old house creaks
as a warm breeze enters
and then leaves, peacefully;
Wire fences stand in disrepair,
gradually giving back
their staked out territory;
This house once stood sturdy
against vicious prairie winds;
Deserted and rickety now,
the old house holds the past
while the land
with its trees and pastures,
holds a promising future.

Jackson's Point

*by **Kenneth Sherman***

The town's promontory tongue,
it juts into Lake Simcoe,
making a division:

to the west there is the protected bay
where a benevolent wind
skims taut sails

and where swimmers breaking surface
laugh, conjuring my own
childhood splashers.

The other side is whitecapped,
a vociferous blue-black,
a snarl of weather.

Today I sit on the weather side
in a cottage that is deserted,
watching through the window

as a ritual circle of boys
on the other
on the bayside pier

swing a girl
in choral countdown
and heave her into deep water.

I put my pen to white paper.

Carry me, tenuous sail,
to that community
of splashers

and to the voice
of a girl
caught in mid-air.

The Home

*by **Rabindranath Tagore***

I paced alone on the road across the field while the sunset was hiding its last gold like a miser.

The daylight sank deeper and deeper into the darkness, and the widowed land, whose harvest had been reaped, lay silent.

Suddenly a boy's shrill voice rose into the sky. He traversed the dark unseen, leaving the track of his song across the hush of the evening.

His village home lay there at the end of the waste land, beyond the sugarcane field, hidden among the shadows of the banana and the slender areca palm, the coconut and the dark green jack-fruit trees.

I stopped for a moment in my lonely way under the starlight, and saw spread before me the darkened earth surrounding with her arms countless homes furnished with cradles and beds, mothers' hearts and evening lamps, and young lives glad with a gladness that knows nothing of its value for the world.

Early Supper

*by **Barbara Howes***

Laughter of children brings
    The kitchen down with laughter.
While the old kettle sings
Laughter of children brings
To a boil all savory things.
    Higher than beam or rafter,
Laughter of children brings
    The kitchen down with laughter.

So ends an autumn day,
    Light ripples on the ceiling,
Dishes are stacked away;
So ends an autumn day,
The children jog and sway
    In comic dances wheeling.
So ends an autumn day,
    Light ripples on the ceiling.

They trail upstairs to bed,
    And night is a dark tower.
The kettle calls: instead
They trail upstairs to bed,
Leaving warmth, the coppery-red
    Mood of their carnival hour.
They trail upstairs to bed,
    And night is a dark tower.

'Mid pleasures and palaces though we may roam
Be it ever so humble, there's no place like home.

— John Howard Payne

Night Journey

*by **Theodore Roethke***

Now as the train bears west,
Its rhythm rocks the earth,
And from my Pullman berth
I stare into the night
While others take their rest.
Bridges of iron lace,
A suddenness of trees,
A lap of mountain mist
All cross my line of sight,
Then a bleak wasted place,
And a lake below my knees.
Full on my neck I feel
The straining at a curve;
My muscles move with steel,
I wake in every nerve.
I watch a beacon swing
From dark to blazing bright;
We thunder through ravines
And gullies washed with light.
Beyond the mountain pass
Mist deepens on the pane;
We rush into a rain
That rattles double glass.
Wheels shake the roadbed stone,
The pistons jerk and shove,
I stay up half the night
To see the land I love.

We Who Were Born

*by **Eiluned Lewis***

We who were born
In country places
Far from cities
And shifting faces,
We have a birthright
No man can sell,
And a secret joy
No man can tell.

For we are kindred
To lordly things:
The wild duck's flight
And the white owl's wings,
The pike and the salmon,
The bull and the horse,
The curlew's cry
And the smell of gorse.

Pride of trees,
Swiftness of streams,
Magic of frost
Have shaped our dreams.
No baser vision
Their spirit fills
Who walk by right
On the naked hills.

She's Called Nova Scotia

by **Rita MacNeil**

She grows on you slowly
The first time you meet
There's just so much beauty
The heart can believe
And you want to stay longer
And she's ever so pleased
You're one of the many who don't want to leave

Chorus
So walk through her green fields
Go down to the sea
The fortune in your eyes
Is more like a dream
She's called Nova Scotia
And she so makes you feel
You've discovered a treasure
No other has seen

It's hard to remember
The places you've been
For once in her presence
She's all that you see
And she cradles you softly
Like a warm gentle breeze
And wins your heart over
With a feeling of peace

Chorus

She welcomes the strangers
From far away shores
While deep down inside her
Some walk through her soul
And at night in her slumber
The winds softly call
And awakens her spirit
That lives in us all

Chorus

High Treason

by **José Emilio Pacheco**
(translated by Alastair Reid)

I do not love my country. Its abstract splendour
is beyond my grasp.
But (although it sounds bad) I would give my life
for ten places in it, for certain people,
seaports, pinewoods, fortresses,
a run-down city, gray, grotesque,
various figures from its history,
mountains
(and three or four rivers)

WRITING FOCUS

W H E R E   I   L I V E

As a class, discuss some of the interesting features and unique characteristics of your community. You might comment on the following: the people, businesses, parks, recreation facilities, local government, restaurants, malls, skyscrapers, bridges, public transportation, and so on. You might also consider some of the features listed below in your discussion.

alleys	escalators	rain and reflections
wildlife	clocks	elegance
rooftops	lights	construction and demolition
litter	snow	fires escapes
poles	colour	sun and shadow
noises	water	signs and posters
elevators	movement	

Working on your own and based on the class discussion, write a **free-verse** poem that represents what is most significant to you about the place where you live.

SENSORY PERCEPTION

Make notes about a place you remember spending a great deal of time: a cottage, a campsite, a relative's home in another country, a shelter, a friend's house, and so on. Include negative as well as positive memories in your notes.

Now, imagine this same place in terms of how you would perceive it if you were to lose one of your senses. Remember, when one sense is cut off, the others become more acute. Find a partner and describe the scene from your memory in terms of only four of the five senses. While one of you is speaking, the other should be making notes.

Write a poem about the scene your partner described to you based on your notes. Your poem should not include any **images** that could only be perceived by the sense that your partner lost. In other words, if your partner lost his or her hearing, your poem should not include words or phrases related to that sense: no "babbling" brooks, no wind "whispering" through the trees, no "loud noises."

Share your poem with your partner and edit it based on his or her suggestions.

WRITING FOCUS

THE JOURNEY

As a group, reread "Night Journey" by Theodore Roethke (p. 133). Imagine taking a trip across Canada by train, bus, or car. Scan through travel books and magazines about Canada for ideas about how various places look. Then, work together to write your own "journey" poem. Try to include a scene from each of the provinces and the Territories. Once everyone is satisfied with the poem, take turns discussing the one place you learned about through your research that you would like to visit some day and describe why you would like to go there.

Home Base

"Shangri-La" is the imaginary land featured in James Hilton's novel *Lost Horizon* (1933). Hilton's creation was so memorable that now the word "Shangrila" is used to mean "an imaginary, remote paradise on earth; a utopia."

Individually, ask at least ten of your classmates to describe one characteristic that each would consider a necessary feature of a fictional "Shangrila." Based on their suggestions, write a free-verse poem. Share your poem with a small group or the whole class. Give this place you have described a name, and discuss the advantages and disadvantages of living there.

Cultural Experiences

everything that a person learns from his or her social group is considered part of that person's "culture." Human beings are the only creatures who have culture. It is not inherited, nor is it instinctive. It is transmitted socially and is passed on and maintained solely through learning.

Most groups, tribes, or societies have their own distinctive cultures. In fact, according to anthropologists, there are over three thousand different cultures in the world, and over seventy common characteristics that exist, in various forms, among them. These shared characteristics include the following:

athletic sports	family	language
bodily adornment	feasting	law
calendar	folklore	marriage
community organization	funeral rites	medicine
cooking	games	music
courtship	gift giving	mythology
dancing	government	numerals
decorative art	greetings	personal names
division of labour	hair styles	property rites
dream interpretation	hospitality	puberty customs
education	housing	religious ritual
ethics	hygiene	tool making
etiquette	joking	trade

Canadians can trace their heritages to almost every country and culture in the world. The following poems will not only help you to recognize the similarities between these cultures, but they will help you to understand and appreciate the differences.

Tonga

*by **Sosefina Tupper** (student)*

"What are you?" a rude girl asked.
      Polynesian:
I am neither white nor black;
hair curly, lips red,
light-skinned, strong-willed.
Born in a land of papaya and mango,
scattered islands and blue oceans,
warm breezes and coconut trees.
Open air markets with friendly people
warm rain water, outdoor showers,
white sand beaches, perpetual sunshine,
turtles, sharks, and wild pigs,
      Polynesian. . . . .

That's what I am, but Who Are You!

How Much Does It Cost?

*by **Mary Fong***

"You should be a poet,"
someone said.
"A traditional Chinese poet."

In grade school
I told my friends
I don't even speak the language
and we use spoons all the time
at home.

Walking in a shopping mall
in downtown Vancouver
a squat Chinese woman
holds a green sweater.
Gae doh chin? she asks.

I look at the tag
count to ten on my Chinese
fingers.
Three, eight, nine, five.
"It costs $38.95,"
I say in English.

I try again
say each number in Chinese
one by one.

Finally I tell her
M'gee ah.

From "The Sullen Shapes of Poems"

*by **Lucy Ng***

Father, in the autumn of your life you embarked
on a 28-day 22-city tour of China. I remember
the names—Beijing, Suzhou, Guilin—the sounds
and shapes delightful to your tongue as you
repeated them to us around the dinner table.
Sometimes dreaming or reading, I think I know
what you must have felt when you climbed that
Great Wall or wandered through those magnificent
rooms, finger-deep in dust. Did you feel the
pain of recognition—thirty years gone—as
you chanced upon this, the undiscovered country,
its imprint in your heart?

The reddish dust of Beijing seeps through our
clothes, chafes at our skin—North American
bred, the disdainful tour guide notes.

It must have been a relief after Hong Kong and
Trinidad (mere islands) to find yourself in the
wide expanse called Canada: British Columbia,
thick fir trees, mountains solid as the back of
your hand. You could buy a house, a piece of
land, plant yourself firmly in the North American
soil. Sometimes you even forgot this was the
second mainland you called home.

A handful of seeds, a little soil, sun.

I Grew Up

by **Lenore Keeshig-Tobias**

I

i grew up on the reserve
thinking it was the most
beautiful place in the world

I grew up thinking
i'm never going
to leave this place

i was a child
a child who would
lie under trees

watching wind's rhythms
sway leafy boughs
back and forth

back and forth
sweeping it seemed
the clouds into great piles

and rocking me as
i snuggled in the grass
like a bug basking in the sun

II

i grew up on the reserve
thinking it was the most
beautiful place in the world

i grew up thinking
i'm never going
to leave this place

i was a child
a child who ran
wild rhythms

through the fields
the streams
the bush

eating berries
cupping cool water
to my wild stained mouth

and hiding in the
treetops with
my friends

III

we used to laugh at teachers and
tourists who referred to
our bush as *forests* or *woods*

forests and *woods*
were places of
fairy-tale text

were places where people,
especially children, got lost
where wild beasts roamed

our bush was where we played
and where the rabbits squirrels
foxes deer and the bear lived

i grew up thinking
i'm never going
to leave this place

i grew up on the reserve
thinking it was the most
beautiful place in the world

Cultural Experiences

Elegy To a Land Lost

by **Kofi Sam**

I dream of the clanging of hoes
And the distant cry of the hawk,
Of farms lush,
And fields green,
Turning brown and dry
In the twinkle of an eye.

I dream of moon-lit nights,
Of the warmth of friends and fires,
Of tales told of old women
And witches,
But suddenly waking to
A biting cold and crushing loneliness.

I dream of fishy scents
And of delicious smells,
Of sitting together with
Huge bowls of steaming soups,
But suddenly fighting
Over a fragment of bread.

I dream of happy laughter,
Of jumping and running faster,
Of hiding behind the hut
And the fun we had.
But suddenly surrounded by
Strange faces and cold stares.

I dream of a bright morning
And of fathers sharing,
Clothes: red, yellow and green,
Of gleaming eyes and envious glances.
But suddenly walking away
In tatters and filth.

I dream of a long journey
Of mothers weeping and children asking,
Of burning heat and numbing cold,
Of howling creatures and unending nights,
Suddenly ending in a land
Of tall buildings and
I, with my hand outstretched.

Hungry Ghost

by **Debjani Chatterjee**

Today I went shopping with my father
after many years. I felt I was back
in time to when I'd follow grandfather
to the market, smelling the spicy scents,
drinking the sights and mingling with the shouts.
Neither buyer nor seller, I would float
like a restless spirit, hungry for life.

The market is bigger. I have grown too.
There are more goods as distances have shrunk.
The prices are higher. I understand
about money and, alas, its bondage
of buyers and sellers. Almost I wish
I was again that hungry ghost, watchful
and floating through the world's noisy bazaar.

An Ear-Piercing Cry

by **Bill Richardson**

Memory's a mystery. We wonder where it dwells.
In the corrugated brain, or locked in every cell?
And can we only recollect our own dull, daily grind?
Or do we access, on occasion, some collective mind?

I rather think the latter for, from time to time, it seems
A world that's surely not my own emerges from my dreams:
A world that's leagues removed from mine: Remote. Exotic. New.
So foreign, yet familiar somehow. Classic *déjà-vu!*

Some ancient tribal recollection rises to the fore,
And I see things that touch me, stir me, to my very core.
I see a father teach his son to wield a deadly spear,
To creep through tangled underbrush, to tell when game is near,

To heave the lance, to pierce the heart, to take the meat and hide.
And when, reluctantly, I wake, when from that place I'm pried,
It seems so real! I can but think that somehow I have tapped
The trunk of common memory, and siphoned off the sap.

And twenty generations hence, when someone like me sleeps —
The tea of antique memory is brewed, and strong and steeped —
He'll kickstart his subconscious, and start revving up *les rêves:*
What will be the potent dreams that future mind will have?

Will he wake with wonderment, or with a sense of awe,
And later at the office tell his colleagues what he saw?:
"I saw a man in middle age and with him was a lad:
The younger was called Jason, and the older was called Dad.

"They both were swathed in denim, and a totem of their tribe
Were caps that bore the logo 'Bluejays' lovingly inscribed.
Each one had a ponytail, though Dad had thinning locks,
And on their feet were army boots that Jason labelled 'Docs.'

"They strode inside a jewellery store. Said Dad, all gruff and fierce:
'The boy and me are here because we want our earlobes pierced.'
A woman with important hair retrieved the piercing tool.
Little Jason sat astride her sacrificial stool.

"He pointed to the left lobe, and she clutched the flap of skin,
Struck with serpent quickness and behold! The stud was in!
And oh, but he was brave! He never screamed or even squirmed.
'Cool!' was all he said, and then to Dad — 'Okay, your turn.'

"Dad was watching carefully. He saw his son impaled.
His brow had turned all sweaty and his face had gone all pale.
His breath was coming rapidly. He had a worried look.
And as he sat astride the stool he trembled and he shook.

"'Left or right?' the priestess asked. Before poor Dad could say
He gagged and then he gurgled and he fainted dead away.
Jason sighed the sigh of one who badly suffers fools.
'Dad,' he groaned. The grown man moaned. 'That's just so, so uncool!'"

Twenty generations hence, when someone tells this dream,
His listeners will scratch their heads, and wonder what it means.
Perhaps someone who's heard of Jung, or studied him at college,
Will mutter something vague about the source of common knowledge,

Of ancient rites of passages, of primitives and magic.
If this is all we leave behind, methinks it's rather tragic.
Worshippers of fashion take a calculated gamble,
Risking the construing of some future Joseph Campbell.

What will archaeologists who excavate the psyche
Make of our reliance on Adidas, Docs and Nikes?
Who will clean the wellspring up? Who dares to dig that deep?
Not me, babe. I'm going to kick my Nikes off and sleep.

CLOSE TO HOME   JOHN McPHERSON

"All right! All right! You've made your point, Dad!
I'll get rid of my earring, I swear!"

In My Backyard

by **Celestino De Iuliis**

I own a house now.
My father sowed his seeds
in his backyard,
and reaped the lettuce and tomatoes.
He had known who he was when
his hands formed the cheese
drawn from the milk of his flock.
Having come here, he was less sure
and worked in factories or construction sites.
He made his own wine and slaughtered still
the Easter Lamb for us
(and for himself too, there's no denying).
He loved what was his own with little show
and fewer words.
The language never yielded to him, strong as he was.
I wrote the numbers out on a sheet
so he could write his cheques,
pay his bills…
My youth was spent in shame of him.
My tiny face would blush, my eyes avert
on parents' night when he would timid come
to ask in broken syntax after me.
In my backyard
I have my grass and flowers
and buy my produce at Dominion.
My eyes avert in shame now
that I ever was that boy.

Cultural Experiences

How I Learned English

by *Gregory Djanikian*

It was an empty lot
Ringed by elms and fir and honeysuckle.
Bill Corson was pitching in his buckskin jacket,
Chuck Keller, fat even as a boy, was on first,
His T-shirt riding up over his gut,
Ron O'Neill, Jim, Dennis, were talking it up
In the field, a blue sky above them
Tipped with cirrus.

        And there I was,
Just off the plane and plopped in the middle
Of Williamsport, Pa. and a neighborhood game,
Unnatural and without any moves,
My notions of baseball and America
Growing fuzzier each time I whiffed.

So it was not impossible that I,
Banished to the outfield and daydreaming
Of water, or a hotel in the mountains,
Would suddenly find myself in the path
Of a ball stung by Joe Barone.
I watched it closing in
Clean and untouched, transfixed
By its easy arc before it hit
My forehead with a thud.

        I fell back,
Dazed, clutching my brow,
Groaning, "Oh my shin, oh my shin,"
And everybody peeled away from me
And dropped from laughter, and there we were,
All of us writhing on the ground for one reason
Or another.

        Someone said "shin" again,

Cultural Experiences

There was a wild stamping of hands on the ground,
A kicking of feet, and the fit
Of laughter overtook me too,
And that was important, as important
As Joe Barone asking me how I was
Through his tears, picking me up
And dusting me off with hands like swatters,
And though my head felt heavy,
I played on till dusk
Missing flies and pop-ups and grounders
And calling out in desperation things like
"Yours" and "take it," but doing all right,
Tugging at my cap in just the right way,
Crouching low, my feet set,
"Hum baby" sweetly on my lips.

▶ My Hands

*by **Takeo Nakano***
(translated by Leatrice Nakano)

As final resting place,
Canada is chosen.
On citizenship paper,
Signing
Hand trembles.

▶ My Hands

*by **Takeo Nakano***
(translated by Robert Y. Kadoguchi)

My hands tremble
As I sign my naturalization papers
Making me a Canadian citizen
And Canada my final resting place.

T I M E   C A P S U L E

Your class has been chosen to make a number of special time capsules to give the people of the future an accurate view of life in the twentieth century. Break into small groups of three to five students each and list those items which you feel represent our way of life. Have a group member record the list. Categorize your items under the following headings:

- ways we dress
- foods we eat
- forms of transportation
- ways we earn a living
- ways we spend our time
- ways we express our feelings
- things we believe in
- heading(s) of your choice

Since your group's time capsule will not be opened for hundreds of years, you must select items which are representative of life in this century. (As an alternative, you may choose to make a time capsule that reflects life in the 1990s.) Only ten items may be included—the container does not count as one of the items—and you must be able to fit them into the capsule.

Remember, one carefully chosen item can convey many pieces of information; for example, a fast food container, a digital watch, an invitation to a wedding. Work together to write a **free-verse** poem about your time capsule that includes the list and a rationale for your choice of objects. If possible, design and build the time capsule and include a copy of your group's poem.

P I C T U R E S   T E L L   S T O R I E S

Find a photograph of an individual or group from another culture. Take five minutes and jot down everything the picture inspires you to see, hear, smell, taste, and touch. Write the rough draft of a free-verse poem based on your cluster of words and **images.** Revise your poem to final draft, ensuring that the finished product conveys your opinions about the lifestyle communicated by the photograph.

> ### COMPUTER TIP
>
> *To make revising easier, input a list of revision strategies in a separate file from your poetry, and call it up on a split screen as you write your next draft.*

C U L T U R A L   C H A N G E

Our Canadian culture is relatively new and is constantly changing. In a small group, discuss the elements and ideas we have "borrowed" from other cultures. You might consider items such as our houses, clothes, shoes, beverages, food, dishes, newspapers, language, and behaviour.

Working on your own, organize your thoughts and feelings about one of the following topics: (i) something that our culture has adopted from another culture; (ii) one of your own experiences regarding cultural roots or cultural change; or, (iii) a topic of your choice that deals with the **theme** of cultural experiences.

Compose a free-verse poem about your topic. If you focus completely on the sensory and emotional experience, you will produce a poem which evokes a strong **mood** or image in the reader's mind.

Cultural Experiences

Write a poem which outlines your perception of what makes up Canadian culture. Read your poem aloud to a small group. Ask for feedback from the group members regarding the ideas presented in your poem. Listen carefully as other group members read their poems on this topic.

Reaching Out

human beings are social creatures. We thrive in an environment where there is contact with other people, no matter how unpleasant or brief our experiences with others may be. It is when we are isolated from human contact that we tend to become depressed, self-absorbed, and pessimistic. Building and sustaining relationships with other people, however, implies a certain risk. If you have ever been hurt by someone in the past, whether it was a friend, relative, teacher, or complete stranger, you may not want to take a chance on anyone else. Not taking a chance, however, may result in you missing out on what could be the greatest friendship, romance, or relationship of your life.

As the poems in this unit show, reaching out to others may not always be easy or pleasant, but the rewards are sometimes worth the effort.

Trouble is a big sieve through which we sift our acquaintances; those who are too big to pass through are friends.

— **Anonymous**

If You Don't Come

by **Marguerite Mack** (student)

The sun will get
smaller and smaller
and the grass won't green
or the trees leaf
and there will be
no flowers or birdsong.

The winds will blow cold
and the nights will be dark
without moonlight or stars

for there will be
no summer here
if you don't come.

What Are Friends For

by **Rosellen Brown**

What are friends for, my mother asks.
A duty undone, visit missed,
casserole unbaked for sick Jane.
Someone has just made her bitter.

Nothing. They are for nothing, friends,
I think. All they do in the end—
they *touch* you. They fill you like music.

Gaining Yardage

*by **Leo Dangel***

The word *friend* never came up
between Arlo and me—we're farm neighbors
who hang around together, walk beans,
pick rocks, and sit on the bench
at football games, weighing the assets
of the other side's cheerleaders.
Tonight we lead 48 to 6, so the coach
figures sending us both in is safe.
I intercept an underthrown pass
only because I'm playing the wrong position
and Arlo is right there to block for me
because he's in the wrong place,
so we gallop up the field, in the clear
until their second-string quarterback
meets us at the five-yard line,
determined to make up for his bad throw.
Arlo misses the block, the guy has me
by the leg and jersey, and going down,
I flip the ball back to Arlo, getting up,
who fumbles, and their quarterback
almost recovers, then bobbles the ball
across the goal line, and our coach,
who told even the guys with good hands
never to mess around with laterals,
must feel his head exploding,
when Arlo and I dive on the ball together
in the end zone and dance and slap
each other on the back.
They give Arlo the touchdown, which rightly
should be mine, but I don't mind,
and I suppose we are friends, and will be,
unless my old man or his decides to move
to another part of the country.

Reaching Out

155

The Competition

*by **Patricia Young***

At times the competition was fierce
between Cheri and me.
Had to be equal in all things.
Neither could bear
that the other could run
faster, pick a raspberry bush cleaner,
that the other's mind could scrape
the bottom of language, discover
the only seven-letter word
comprised entirely
of consonants.

Take skipping, take double dutch.
If she jumped 421 times without stopping
I'd jump 422, maybe 423, before collapsing
on the pavement.

Compared report cards, number of cavities,
valentines. Take boys.

We don't need them, we've got each other.

Dear Cheri: your cupped hands held me like water.
Can't remember when we began slipping
through each other's fingers.

First Love

*by **Joan A. Hamilton***

Like countless others
long before your time,
your mission darkened
by a dozen doubts,
you sidle up,
inch closer to the door.

Time's deft hand is visible
molding adolescence
from shapeless puberty
that bares the rawness
of a first-time love.

"Is Thea in?" you ask.

Not waiting for an answer
and scuffling sneakered feet,
you sputter on, "you know,
I mean, I think
we sorta have a date."

PEANUTS reprinted by permission of UFS, Inc.

Sonnet 18

*by **William Shakespeare***

Shall I compare thee to a summer's day?
Thou art more lovely and more temperate:
Rough winds do shake the darling buds of May,
And summer's lease hath all too short a date:
Sometime too hot the eye of heaven shines,
And often is his gold complexion dimmed;
And every fair from fair sometimes declines,
By chance or nature's changing course untrimmed;
But thy eternal summer shall not fade,
Nor lose possession of that fair thou owest;
Nor shall Death brag thou wander'st in his shade,
When in eternal lines to time thou growest:
    So long as men can breathe, or eyes can see,
    So long lives this, and this gives life to thee.

Reaching Out

It's Raining in Love

*by **Richard Brautigan***

I don't know what it is,
but I distrust myself
when I start to like a girl
    a lot.

It makes me nervous.
I don't say the right things
or perhaps I start
    to examine,
        evaluate,
            compute
    what I am saying.

If I say, "Do you think it's going to rain?"
and she says, "I don't know,"
I start thinking: Does she really like me?

In other words
I get a little creepy.

A friend of mine once said,
"It's twenty times better to be friends
    with someone
than it is to be in love with them."

I think he's right and besides,
it's raining somewhere, programming flowers
and keeping snails happy.
    That's all taken care of.

    BUT
if a girl likes me a lot
and starts getting real nervous
and suddenly begins asking me funny questions

and looks sad if I give the wrong answers
and she says things like,
"Do you think it's going to rain?"
and I say, "It beats me,"
and she says, "Oh,"
and looks a little sad
at the clear blue California sky,
I think: Thank God, it's you, baby, this time
    instead of me.

▶ The Forcefields

*by **Robert Priest***

There was a girl with a forcefield
it made her feel protected
but the forcefield had a malfunction
that couldn't be corrected

she fell in love with a boy named Nerx
who had a forcefield too
who likewise fell in love with her
but what could these two do?

she couldn't turn her forcefield off
and neither alas could he
and so these two could never hug
though they loved eternally

but still they loved as lovers do
though the force kept them apart
and though they loved from far away
they loved with all their hearts

Cold Bus Ride

*by **Glen Sorestad***

We ride the bus together
    this cold January morning,
clothed heavily in silence,
    strangers sharing a seat,
each of us benumbed
    by bitter wind,
reluctant and withdrawn,
    no desire to speak,
or even force a smile
    in our seclusion.
We are private and defensive,
    our need for words
frozen, left behind
    at wind-torn bus stops.

Only when our bus halts
    and we both must rise
from the same seat do we
    smile at each other,
tentative acknowledgement
    that we have shared
fifteen minutes of our lives
    close to one another
sharing nothing more
    than body warmth.

Pterodactyls

*by **Marjorie L. Sallee***

Never trust a teacher with tantalizing eyes
Or pterodactyls on his tie,
Who collects strange toys
And bids on junk at auctions.
He will pull you into poetry
And hook your mind on literary history.
Then, when you need to tune him out,
You can't. And years later
His voice still haunts you
Sending you in search of
Books you haven't read yet.

Those pterodactyls might have warned
Of the persistence of his instruction.
Their species may have vanished,
But like the poets in the book
He made them breathe again for us.

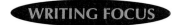

WRITING FOCUS

S I G N I F I C A N T   O T H E R

Take ten minutes and, without stopping, write whatever comes into your head regarding various types of human relationships. If you get stuck, write the last word over and over again until your mind "clicks" into another idea.

Select one of the relationships on your list that is particularly important to you. It might be a relationship you have with a friend, a sibling, a parent or guardian, a teacher, a coach. Write a poem that describes what you cherish most about this relationship. Try to incorporate dialogue into your poem.

As an alternative, you might select a passage of text from your favourite novel, short story, or play that describes a relationship between two characters. Try to communicate the feelings expressed in the passage in the form of a **free-verse** poem.

WRITING FOCUS

S T R A N G E R S   A M O N G   U S

With another student, observe and make notes about the different ways strangers interact with one another. Your focus should not be on one particular person, but on the brief encounters people have every day with those around them; for example, at shopping malls, on buses, and so on. Consider the following in your observations: are people generally friendly with strangers? are they rude or polite? do they appear considerate of others' feelings or needs? do they strive to maintain a certain range of personal space? what kind of body language do they use in the company of strangers? Discuss the results of your observations with the rest of the class.

Based on the class discussion, write a poem about the topic of interaction among strangers.

Alternatively, research and write a poem about Canada's relationship with other countries. What, for example, is our role in world politics? How do other countries perceive Canadians? If you have lived in another country, include your experiences and opinions in your poem.

Reaching Out

WRITING FOCUS

R O L E - P L A Y I N G

In a small group, discuss the emotions that might surface in a romantic relationship; for example, love, jealousy, anger, sympathy, and so on. Outline a scenario for a telephone conversation in which two people who are romantically involved are expressing some of these emotions. (Whether your characters are real or fictional, be sure to establish some background information for both of them: name, age, economic status, hobbies, interests, education, and so on.) Take turns role-playing the telephone conversation in front of the rest of the group.

> **COMPUTER TIP**
>
> *The visual presentation of your poem can alter its meaning. Experiment with different styles and sizes of type to emphasize your meaning visually. For example, the word "loud" in a poem might be input using large, boldfaced letters.*

Once everyone has had a chance to play one of the roles, work on your own to write a poem about the incident. Use **metaphors, similes,** and **images** that appeal to the senses and convey the intensity of the emotion.

SHARING AND PUBLISHING

Write a poem in the form of a letter to someone with whom you share a special relationship. Revise it until you are comfortable with the thoughts and feelings being expressed, then mail it to the person.

Reaching Out

Visions of Reality

most of us learn to deal with reality in a logical and controlled manner—even though everyone's vision of reality is different. There are times, however, when we distort reality to suit our own needs. Have you ever heard what you wanted someone to say rather than what the person actually said? When an individual has an accurate perception of reality, it will not be distorted by needs or wishes.

Most people are eager to learn about the reality of someone else's life, especially if there is an aspect to that person's reality that we can relate to or share. That is why news reports and "reality-based" programming are so popular. The following poems deal with issues to which you may be able to relate: divorce, driving, illness, love, education, and cruelty. Don't be surprised if the people and situations presented in these poems mirror your own vision of reality.

Human kind cannot bear very much reality.

— T.S. Eliot

The Orchard

by *Helen Van Dongen* (student)

a wise man
once said —
life is a
cherry…
you take the
fruit
with the pits
and if you
break your
back
trying to find
the ripest
fruit
inside you'll find
the biggest
pits…
I think
he's right.

We live in a fantasy world, a world of illusion.

The great task in life is to find reality.

— **Iris Murdoch**

A Case of Divorce

*by **Dwayne Edmundson** (student)*

All my friends
live in this town
enemies, too—
Ten years of escape routes
secret hideouts
and a super trike path
through Cottwell's field.
This town,
it's everything I know.
Sid's 21 flavours of ice-cream
mmn…
orange sherbert.
And the pinball machine
at the confectionary.
And here I am
packing china,
emptying water beds
leaving—
because my mother is…

On Receiving My Driver's Licence

*by **Karmyn Lewis** (student)*

Freedom, exquisite total freedom;
Superiority over the "younger" generation;
My first set of keys;
That tingling sensation as foot hits accelerator;
The sudden "rush" when someone asks for a ride.

Humiliation with that first speeding ticket;
Terror at the sudden impact of a car accident;
Responsibility of getting others home safely;
The promise not to drink and drive.

The Big Years

by *Jo Lena*

I don't want
to be
a teenager
any more.

For a long time
I couldn't wait.

I'm ten
and being a
teenager was
a big deal.

Fast cars
late night T.V.
spending money
my own room
big kid places.

But yesterday
that all stopped.

Four teenagers
killed my dog.

He was on a sidewalk,
my dog, Pal, was on the
sidewalk

Four teenagers
in a car
drove up
over the curb

to hit him.

They were laughing,
I saw them
in a red car,
four teenagers.

I buried Pal
out in the ferns
behind the creek
where ten-year-olds
and their dogs
go to play.

Teenagers never
go near the place.

First Frost

by **Andrei Voznesensky**
(translated by Stanley Kunitz)

A girl is freezing in a telephone booth,
huddled in her flimsy coat,
her face stained by tears
and smeared with lipstick.

She breathes on her thin little fingers.
Fingers like ice. Glass beads in her ears.

She has to beat her way back alone
down the icy street.

First frost. A beginning of losses.
The first frost of telephone phrases.

It is the start of winter glittering on her cheek,
the first frost of having been hurt.

Parents Just Don't Understand

(an excerpt)   by ***Jazzy Jeff & the Fresh Prince***

You know parents are the same
No matter time nor place
They don't understand that us kids
Are going to make some mistakes
So to you, all the kids all across the land
There's no need to argue
Parents just don't understand
I remember one year
My mom took me school shopping
It was me, my brother, my mom, oh, my pop, and my little sister
All hopped in the car
We headed downtown to the Gallery Mall
My mom started bugging with the clothes she chose
I didn't say nothing at first
I just turned up my nose
She said, "What's wrong? This shirt cost $20"
I said, "Mom, this shirt is plaid with a butterfly collar!"
The next half hour was the same old thing
My mother buying me clothes from 1963
And then she lost her mind and did the ultimate
I asked her for Adidas and she bought me Zips!
I said, "Mom, what are you doing, you're ruining my rep"
She said, "You're only sixteen, you don't have a rep yet"
I said, "Mom, let's put these clothes back, please"
She said, "No, you go to school to learn not for a fashion show"
I said, "This isn't Sha Na Na, come on Mom, I'm not Bowzer
Mom, please put back the bell-bottom Brady Bunch trousers
But if you don't want to I can live with that but
You gotta put back the double-knit reversible slacks"
She wasn't moved—everything stayed the same
Inevitably the first day of school came
I thought I could get over, I tried to play sick

But my mom said, "No, no way, uh-uh, forget it"

There was nothing I could do, I tried to relax

I got dressed up in those ancient artifacts

And when I walked into school, it was just as I thought

The kids were cracking up laughing at the clothes Mom bought

And those who weren't laughing still had a ball

Because they were pointing and whispering

As I walked down the hall

I got home and told my Mom how my day went

She said, "If they were laughing you don't need them,

'Cause they're not good friends"

For the next six hours I tried to explain to my Mom

That I was gonna have to go through this about 200 more times

So to you all the kids all across the land

There's no need to argue

Parents just don't understand

▶ Paul Hewitt

*by **Mel Glenn***

Please, sir, I don't mean to be disrespectful.

I did raise my hand.

I mean, who cares if Macbeth becomes a monster,

If Huck Finn rescues Jim,

If Willie Loman never finds happiness?

They're just characters in books.

What have they got to do with me?

I mean, I'm never going hunting for white whales.

I'm never going to fight in the Civil War.

And I certainly don't live in the Dust Bowl.

Tell me instead how to

Make money, pick up girls.

Then maybe I'll listen.

You got any books that deal with real life?

Preposterous

*by **Jim Hall***

At fifteen Jean Calvin made a list:
Best Legs, Sexiest Smile, Best Muscles,
all the rest. She had the right to judge us
since she was Most Buxom herself,
Most Dreamed About,
Most Discussed When Flesh Came Up.

I sat behind her in Civics that aromatic year
and whispered jokes and tried to breathe her hair.
For all that I won Wittiest. Wittiest.
And was runner-up for Best Legs on a Short Boy.

She posted it and overnight her picks
for All-round Sexiest, Perkiest Buns, Dreamiest,
drew flocks around their lockers.
And everything I said was suddenly preposterous
and clever. I could roll my eyes that June
and break up Biology.

It wasn't what I wanted, but I took it.
I wanted to be one of those who could whisper
in Jean Calvin's hair and make her wheel and slap
and turn back around with a secret smile.
I wanted a gift: Best Voice, Bedroomiest Eyes,
some rousing inherited trait. Not this,
this Wittiest, which makes me work so hard,
so everlastingly, to keep Jean Calvin entertained.

© 1994, Washington Post Writers Group.
Reprinted with permission.

WRITING FOCUS

D A Y   I N   T H E   L I F E

Make notes about your observations and experiences during the course of a typical school day. Develop these notes into a **free-verse** poem. Your poem might include references to peer pressure, handling homework assignments and exams, extra-curricular activities, social events, and so on. The following guidelines might help:

- Review your notes.
- Visualize the scene you want to write about.
- Write down the **images** that occur to you.
- Include images that appeal to the senses.
- Identify places where sentences should break into lines, and lines into stanzas.
- Alter the wording, if appropriate. Consider the "sound" as well as the "meaning."
- Reread your poem.
- Prepare a final draft.

> ## C O M P U T E R   T I P
>
> Improve the **diction** of the poems in your writing folder by using the "search-and-replace" or "change" command. Search for common words such as "good," "nice," "small," and see how your poems sound when these words are replaced with synonyms. Make sure to use a duplicate file of your work.

R E A L I T Y   I N   T H E   M E D I A

Working with a partner or small group, discuss the similarities and differences between reality as it is experienced firsthand, and the media's presentation of reality. You might focus on advertising campaigns, television programs, or magazines that are targeted at your age group.

Working on your own, write a poem that outlines your thoughts and opinions about the media's presentation of reality.

WRITING FOCUS

M E M O R A B L E   M O M E N T

Write a poem about one of the following topics: your most embarrassing moment; a moment of glory; a pleasant experience that seemed real but was actually a dream; a painful experience that you wished was a dream.

Your poem should describe the feelings you experienced during your encounter with reality.

SHARING AND PUBLISHING

Obtain permission to display on school property a mural that is comprised of words taken from a poem written by each of your classmates, as well as appropriate pictures or illustrations representing the reality of life at your school. Or, you could submit a photograph of the mural for inclusion in the school yearbook or newspaper.

Visions of Reality

Active Life

how did athletic activities begin? Did a caveman challenge his neighbour one day to a spear-tossing contest? Maybe some cavekids started hitting a rock with a pterodactyl bone.

Although no one really knows what the first athletic activity was, archaeologists can tell us that many sports—wrestling, archery, horseback riding, rowing, running—are thousands of years old. The first true Olympic Games were held in 776 B.C.E. at Olympia in ancient Greece, and were held every four years in the summer to honour the god Zeus. The Games tested strength, skill, speed, and endurance. In C.E. 394, Olympic athleticism had declined to barbarism, and a decree was issued that prohibited the celebration of the Games of Olympia. The revival of the modern Olympic Games did not take place until 1894 in Paris. The first Olympic Winter Games were held in France in 1924.

As the poems you are about to read suggest, an active lifestyle is important, not only for health reasons, but for the skills, self-confidence, camaraderie, and sense of goal-setting and achievement that involvement in an activity can foster.

The Race

*by **Kirsty Foot** (student)*

With two laps left,
and trailing another athlete;
solemnly grunting and breathing,
my blood is pumping.
And soon,
my legs feel numb.
All I can do is go faster,
watching the ground swirl by,
the heat,
    the yelling,
        the sun
            in my eyes.
And then, there is the finish line
bright, white, and shining.
It divides us between winner
and loser.
I run,
and start to catch up,
breathing,
swallowing air
    and dust
        and time,
time just goes on forever.
Then,
it happens,
I fall
on the gravel.
And then,
I look up;
to see the winner passing me by.

The Last Shot

by ***Darryl Adamko*** (student)

A feeling of solitude.
Only the humming of an old fan
Dares destroy the silence.

He rubs his
Raw
Red
Hands on his pants,
Numb from the exposure to cold,
Concentrating on the broom constantly.

Gripping the rock,
Cold and hard,
Unresponsive—
Slide
Slow down
Launch it forward,
A satellite on its solid space.

The call for the sweep
Tears the tension.
The rink jumps to life.
Keep it going!
Don't stop now!
Let it curl—
Maneuver it in.
Bring it on—
Two more feet—
    On
        The
            Button!

A Dive

*by **Mary Jo Donnelly** (student)*

There is a low murmur,
Among the many spectators.
I forget the noise
As mentally,
I prepare for my dive.
Seconds pass.
I lift my arms.
Bouncing off the rough surface,
I bend towards the water far below.
And then straight down, down, down,
Like a missile, I cut into
the blue depths, which swallow me.

PEANUTS reprinted by permission of UFS, Inc.

Prediction: School P.E.

by *Isabel Joshlin Glaser*

Someday
when the baseball's
    hurtling
like some UFO,
    blazing
like some mad thing
    toward me
        in outfield

I *won't* gasp
and dodge. Oh, no!
Instead, I'll be
calmer than calm
    —so la-de-da!—
I'll just reach out
    like a *pro*
and catch it and—quick!—
    throw to second.
And everyone will say, "Hooray!
Natalie made a double-play!"
Some day.

Analysis of Baseball

*by **May Swenson***

It's about
the ball,
the bat,
and the mitt.
Ball hits
bat, or it
hits mitt.
Bat doesn't
hit ball, bat
meets it.
Ball bounces
off bat, flies
air, or thuds
ground (dud)
or it
fits mitt.

Bat waits
for ball
to mate.
Ball hates
to take bat's
bait. Ball
flirts, bat's
late, don't
keep the date.
Ball goes in
(thwack) to mitt,
and goes out
(thwack) back
to mitt.

Ball fits
mitt, but
not all
the time.
Sometimes
ball gets hit
(pow) when bat
meets it,
and sails
to a place
where mitt
has to quit
in disgrace.
That's about
the bases
loaded,
about 40,000
fans exploded.

It's about
the ball,
the bat,
the mitt,
the bases
and the fans.
It's done
on a diamond,
and for fun.
It's about
home, and it's
about run.

The Jump Shooter

by **Dennis Trudell**

The way the ball
hung there
against the blue or purple

one night last week
across town
at the playground where

I had gone to spare
my wife
from the mood I'd swallowed

and saw in the dusk
a stranger
shooting baskets a few

years older maybe
thirty-five
and overweight a little

beer belly saw him
shooting there
and joined him didn't

ask or anything simply
went over
picked off a rebound

and hooked it back up
while he
smiled I nodded and for

ten minutes or so we
took turns
taking shots and the thing

is neither of us said
a word
and this fellow who's

too heavy now and slow
to play
for any team still had

the old touch seldom
ever missed
kept moving further out

and finally his t-shirt
a gray
and fuzzy blur I stood

under the rim could
almost hear
a high school cheer

begin and fill a gym
while wooden
bleachers rocked he made

three in a row from
twenty feet
moved back two steps

faked out a patch
of darkness
arched another one and

the way the ball
hung there
against the blue or purple

then suddenly filled
the net
made me wave goodbye

breathe deeply and begin
to whistle
as I walked back home.

Hockey

*by **Scott Blaine***

The ice is smooth, smooth, smooth.
The air bites to the center
Of warmth and flesh, and I whirl.
It begins in a game…
The puck swims, skims, veers,
Goes leading my vision
Beyond the chasing reach of my stick.

The air is sharp, steel-sharp.
I suck needles of breathing,
And feel the players converge.
It grows to a science…
We clot, break, drive,
Electrons in motion
In the magnetic pull of the puck.

The play is fast, fierce, tense.
Sticks click and snap like teeth
Of wolves on the scent of a prey.
It ends in the kill…
I am one of the pack in a mad,
Taut leap of desperation
In the wild, slashing drive for the goal.

Ink runs from the corners of my mouth.
There is no happiness like mine.
I have been eating poetry.

— Mark Strand

The Skaters

*by **John Gould Fletcher***

Black swallows swooping or gliding
In a flurry of entangled loops and curves,
The skaters skim over the frozen river.
And the grinding click of their skates as they impinge
      upon the surface,
Is like the brushing together of thin wing-tips of
      silver.

WRITING FOCUS

POETRY IN MOTION

In a small group, list and describe at least ten athletic activities that collectively your group members have had. Examples should include both the ordinary and the momentous.

From the list, select one of the group members' experiences that seemed especially vivid to you. Working on your own, write a poem about his or her experience. Experiment with some of the following poetic devices to make your poem more interesting: **alliteration**, **metaphor**, **onomatopoeia**, **personification**, **simile**. Then, share your poem with the person who had the experience.

WRITING FOCUS

SPORTS JARGON

People involved with sports tend to use jargon to describe their experiences. Jargon consists of terminology unique to a

COMPUTER TIP

The best ideas sometimes don't surface when you need them. Try keeping an "idea file" in your computer. Every time you hear a word or phrase that appeals to you, record it in the file for reference later.

Active Life

specific group of people: in this case, athletes. Select one of your favourite sports and list examples of the jargon associated with it. You may want to consult articles or broadcasts about the sport for ideas.

Compose the first draft of a **free-verse** poem, using some of these examples to make it interesting. Revise your poem and read it aloud to your classmates. Challenge them to guess what sport your poem is about.

WRITING FOCUS

THE OLYMPOETICS

With the class divided into groups, each group should select a different school sporting event or extra-curricular activity. Attend the event as a group, if possible, and individually make notes on what occurs.

Summarize each group members' notes into one detailed account of the event, then work together to write a poem in the **form** of a sports report. Once you are satisfied with your poem, take turns reading it on videotape. Choose the best version and submit it to your teacher for inclusion in a whole-class videotaped sports broadcast titled "The Olympoetics."

SHARING AND PUBLISHING

Work together to publish a class newspaper that features, among other items, at least one "active life" poem written by every student in the class. You will need to select a managing editor to coordinate the various activities: photography, typesetting, layout.

Choose an appropriate title for your newspaper and, if possible, distribute copies of it around the school.

The Natural World

throughout history, human existence has been deeply embedded in and dependent on nature. When plants and animals were plentiful, humans flourished. When drought and famine struck, our numbers fell accordingly. We remain every bit as dependent on nature today, even though days and weeks may pass when we barely even notice it.

Poets, however, are often acutely aware of the world around them. Their curiosity leads them to observe, to explore, to question the visible world that exists independent of human interference. Many poems have been inspired by the natural world. If you are interested in nature, go outside and experience it firsthand. Then, write about what you see, hear, smell, taste, and touch.

I think the coming of spring, the stars overhead, the first snowfall and so on are gifts for a young child, a young poet.

— Sylvia Plath

Autumn Revenge

*by **Leyla Demir** (student)*

We
rake you
behind our
priorities, and
talk about you behind
your back. We neglect
your beautiful shades of
green to red. In return you
are cold and unforgiving.
You blow your harsh words into
our coats, and slap our hats
onto the roads. No longer
can you stand the criticism.
Your words are quiet,
your actions
are
loud.

Siamese Fighting Fish

*by **Jason Benn** (student)*

The fish glides gracefully across the tank
His unblinking eyes stare bold and blank
His fantail flaps like a flag
Proud in his rainbow-plated armor
    he hovers majestically over a sea of gem-like gravel
Then, instinctively, it arches into a warrior's stance
With one swift movement it lunges at its prey
After viciously tearing it apart
    it feasts on its remains like a barbarian.

Uninvited

*by **Maureen Hillaby** (student)*

Listen.
It dies
and comes to life once more,
an uninvited visitor
haunting the late August woods.
It wanders
through the trees
leaving headless stems
of dandelions.
It scatters
their small grey thoughts
    across
        the open
           field.

Until I Saw the Sea

*by **Lilian Moore***

Until I saw the sea
I did not know
that wind
could wrinkle water so.

I never knew
that sun
could splinter a whole sea of blue.

Nor
did I know before,
a sea breathes in and out
upon a shore.

The Lonely Land

*by **A.J.M. Smith***

Cedar and jagged fir
uplift sharp barbs
against the gray
and cloud-piled sky;
and in the bay
blown spume and windrift
and thin, bitter spray
snap
at the whirling sky;
and the pine trees
lean one way.

A wild duck calls
to her mate,
and the ragged
and passionate tones
stagger and fall,
and recover,
and stagger and fall,
on these stones—
are lost
in the lapping of water
on smooth, flat stones.

This is a beauty
of dissonance,
this resonance
of stony strand,
this smoky cry
curled over a black pine
like a broken
and wind-battered branch
when the wind
bends the tips of the pines
and curdles the sky
from the north.

This is the beauty
of strength
broken by strength
and still strong.

Canadian January Night

*by **Alden Nowlan***

Ice storm: the hill
a pyramid of black crystal
down which the cars
slide like phosphorescent beetles
while I, walking backwards in obedience
to the wind, am possessed
of the fearful knowledge
my compatriots share
but almost never utter:
this is a country
where a man can die
              simply from being
caught outside.

Sea-Gulls

*by **E.J. Pratt***

For one carved instant as they flew,
The language had no simile—
Silver, crystal, ivory
Were tarnished. Etched upon the horizon blue,
The frieze must go unchallenged, for the lift
And carriage of the wings would stain the drift
Of stars against a tropic indigo
Or dull the parable of snow.

Now settling one by one
Within green hollows or where curled
Crests caught the spectrum from the sun,
A thousand wings are furled.
No clay-born lilies of the world
Could blow as free
As those wild orchids of the sea.

The Tyger

by **William Blake**

Tyger! Tyger! burning bright
In the forests of the night,
What immortal hand or eye
Could frame thy fearful symmetry?

In what distant deeps or skies
Burnt the fire of thine eyes?
On what wings dare he aspire?
What the hand dare seize the fire?

And what shoulder, & what art,
Could twist the sinews of thy heart?
And when thy heart began to beat,
What dread hand? & what dread feet?

What the hammer? what the chain?
In what furnace was thy brain?
What the anvil? what dread grasp
Dare its deadly terrors clasp?

When the stars threw down their spears,
And water'd heaven with their tears,
Did he smile his work to see?
Did he who made the Lamb make thee?

Tyger! Tyger! burning bright
In the forests of the night,
What immortal hand or eye,
Dare frame thy fearful symmetry?

"I just love it when you quote Blake."

EDWARD FRASCINO

Snake

*by **Emily Dickinson***

A narrow fellow in the grass
Occasionally rides;
You may have met him,—did you not?
His notice sudden is.

The grass divides as with a comb,
A spotted shaft is seen;
And then it closes at your feet
And opens further on.

He likes a boggy acre,
A floor too cool for corn.
Yet when a child, and barefoot,
I more than once, at morn,

Have passed, I thought, a whip-lash
Unbraiding in the sun,—
When, stopping to secure it,
It wrinkled, and was gone.

Several of nature's people
I know, and they know me;
I feel for them a transport
Of cordiality;

But never met this fellow,
Attended or alone,
Without a tighter breathing,
And zero at the bone.

Wolves

by John Haines

Last night I heard wolves howling,
their voices coming from afar
over the wind-polished ice—so much
brave solitude in that sound.

They are death's snowbound sailors;
they know only a continual
drifting between moonlit islands,
their tongues licking the stars.

But they sing as good seamen should,
and tomorrow the sun will find them,
yawning and blinking
the snow from their eyelashes.

Their voices rang through the frozen
water of my human sleep,
blown by the night wind
with the moon for an icy sail.

In the Field Forever

by Robert Wallace

Sun's a roaring dandelion, hour by hour.
Sometimes the moon's a scythe, sometimes a silver flower.
But the stars! all night long the stars are clover,
Over, and over, and over!

WRITING FOCUS

USING IMAGERY

Poets often use **imagery** to paint pictures in the mind of the reader. In this activity, you will be painting your own word picture about nature in the form of a **lyric** poem.

The Natural World

Begin by sitting quietly in an outdoor setting. Observe and make notes about the sights, smells, and sounds of the entire landscape. Then, scan the following list and highlight those sensory experiences which could be incorporated into your poem. Your nature poem should communicate the feelings and impressions you had during your adventure outdoors.

- Recall when you saw something
  - …bright
  - …dark
  - …mesmerizing
  - …colourful
  - …touching
  - …amusing

- Recall when you tasted something
  - …sour
  - …sweet
  - …bitter
  - …spicy
  - …for the first time
  - …you were dared to eat

- Recall when you smelled
  - …burning leaves
  - …a favourite food
  - …pine needles
  - …freshly mown grass
  - …something scorched
  - …someone's cologne

- Recall when you touched
  - …a sponge full of water
  - …a young animal
  - …something smooth
  - …something rough
  - …ice
  - …hot sand

- Recall when you heard
  - …a whisper
  - …running water
  - …an ear-piercing sound
  - …a memorable voice
  - …a musical instrument
  - …rain on the window

Revise your poem with the help of a peer editor.

WRITING FOCUS

S E A S O N A L   C O L O U R S

Choose a season and list as many **images** associated with it as you can. Scan your list of images and write down one colour that you associate with each image. You may want to ask other classmates what colours they associate with certain images. Circle the one colour that appears most often on your list.

Write a poem about your season in which the name of the colour is frequently repeated throughout. As you write, keep reflecting on the personal associations that particular colour holds for you.

WRITING FOCUS

FACTS AND FEELINGS

Work with a small group and reread all the poems in this unit that focus on an animal. Choose one of the poems and discuss any scientific information about the animal that the poet reveals; for example, physical characteristics, behaviour patterns, and so on. How does the poet appeal to the reader's senses and emotional response? Have a group member record the comments and ensure everyone contributes to the discussion.

Go over the discussion notes and list those words and phrases which convey contrasting statements about the animal. Then, work on your own to write a poem that conveys your personal feelings about the animal. Share your poem with the group and identify the various feelings your classmates had toward the same animal.

SHARING AND PUBLISHING

Research the flora and fauna of another country. If you have lived in another country, volunteer to share some of the "natural" features of that country through interviews, open class discussion, and so on.

Share your newly acquired knowledge of geography and science (biology, botany, zoology) in a poem. If you are asked to do a research project on another country for your geography class, you may want to incorporate your poem into that project.

Reflections

reflection is the act of thinking, so it follows that the reflective form of writing deals with the communication of ideas. Reflective writing, which frequently takes the form of poetry, presents deep thought and meaning. In a reflective poem, the writer often moves from a state of contemplation of an idea or a situation, to a state of understanding. Such poems show that the poet has learned something, has grasped the significance of a concept.

There is a certain contentment, or at least resolve, at the end of a reflective poem that seems to suggest that giving form to one's thoughts is therapeutic. By expressing the problem, issue, or idea, the poet has gained a new perspective, and the problem may not seem so troublesome or overwhelming anymore. Writing this type of poem is almost like talking with a friend who acts as a sounding board. Reflective writing gives us an opportunity to gain further insight into who we are and where we fit in. Some of the poems that follow reveal these insights, while others simply describe a special, reflective moment.

Think wrongly, if you please,
but in all cases think for yourself.
— **Doris Lessing**

My Six-line Poem

by *Kerri Bugbee* (student)

As I sit amongst
Crumpled dreams that I have
Tried to scrunch
Into a six-line poem,
I think of Emily Dickinson
And how poems come
Easier
    and easier
        and easier
For some people.

I think of all the thoughts,
And dreams,
And why they never
Turn into words,
But stay in my mind.
I have to think
    harder
        and harder
          and harder
To accomplish this difficult task.

Try to scrunch life
Into a six-line poem.

Far Away

by **Osiaol** (student)

…Soulfulness
is in me
as I harmonize the spell
of your name
under the shadow of evening stars—
for they form some distance
between us,
and my soul
always bears evening shadow's
burden.

The Rider

by **Naomi Shihab Nye**

A boy told me
if he rollerskated fast enough
his loneliness couldn't catch up to him,

the best reason I ever heard
for trying to be a champion.

What I wonder tonight
pedaling hard down King William Street
is if it translates to bicycles.

A victory! To leave your loneliness
panting behind you on some street corner
while you float free into a cloud of sudden azaleas,
luminous pink petals that have never felt loneliness,
no matter how slowly they fell.

Reflections

From "The Diary of a Young Girl"

*by **Anne Frank***
(translated by B.M. Mooyaard)

It's really a wonder
that I haven't dropped all my ideals,
because they seem so absurd
and impossible to carry out.
Yet I keep them,
because in spite of everything,
I still believe
that people are really good at heart.
I simply can't build up my hopes
on a foundation
consisting of confusion, misery, and death.
I see the ever approaching thunder,
which will destroy us too.
I can feel the sufferings of millions and yet,
if I look up into the heavens,
I think that it will all come right,
that this cruelty too will end,
and that peace and tranquillity will return again.

In the meantime, I must uphold my ideals,
for perhaps the time will come when I shall be able to carry them out.

On a Sunny Evening

Anonymous

On a purple, sun-shot evening
Under wide-flowering chestnut trees
Upon the threshold full of dust
Yesterday, today, the days are all like these.

Trees flower forth in beauty,
Lovely too their very wood all gnarled and old
That I am half afraid to peer
Into their crowns of green and gold.

The sun has made a veil of gold
So lovely that my body aches.
Above, the heavens shriek with blue
Convinced I've smiled by some mistake.
The world's abloom and seems to smile.
I want to fly but where, how high?
If in barbed wire, things can bloom
Why couldn't I? I will not die!

A moment's thinking is an hour in words.

— Thomas Hood

Me as My Grandmother

by **Rosemary Aubert**

Sometimes
I look up quickly
and see for an instant
her face
in my mirror,
random tightness
turns my mouth
into a facsimile of hers,
eyes caught oddly
in the glass
make me
into her
looking at me.

Now that she's dead,
I understand
that it is right
that I should age
and wrinkle into her.
It brings her back,
it puts me into
the cycle of family.
We look at all time
with just that
one same face.

The Unending Sky

by **John Masefield**

I could not sleep for thinking of the sky,
    The unending sky, with all its million suns
Which turn their planets everlastingly
    In nothing, where the fire-haired comet runs.
If I could sail that nothing, I should cross
    Silence and emptiness with dark stars passing;
Then, in the darkness, see a point of gloss
    Burn to a glow, and glare, and keep massing,
And rage into a sun with wandering planets,
    And drop behind; and then, as I proceed,
See his last light upon his last moon's granites
    Die to a dark that would be night indeed:
Night where my soul might sail a million years
In nothing, not even Death, not even tears.

We often go through life trying to figure things out, trying to understand relationships between things, trying to solve mysteries. We may look at the world and ask, "Why are things like that?" Or, we may consider a more personal situation and ask ourselves the question, "Why can't I…?"

In a small group, discuss some aspects of life in general—or of your life in particular—that puzzle or concern you, or that you feel are unfair. Make notes during the discussion. You might also scan your journal for places where you expressed confusion or concern about an aspect of life.

Individually, select one of the topics from your discussion and organize your questions and ideas into the rough draft of a brief poem. Reflect on what you find difficult to comprehend and express those thoughts in your poem. Use the following guidelines to revise and prepare a final draft: Is my poem a sincere treatment of the topic? Which words should be omitted, substituted, or rearranged to make my poem more concise? Are the line arrangements effective?

Once you are satisfied with your poem, rewrite it in your journal.

WRITING FOCUS

W O N D E R S T R U C K

Reflective writing often stems from an author's sense of wonder. With a small group, research and write a poem about one of the Seven Wonders of the Ancient World, or anything in the modern world that fills you with a sense of awe and wonder. Your poem might begin with a stanza that outlines your sense of wonder and end with a stanza that outlines what you learned about the topic from your research.

Share the poem with your classmates and answer any questions they may have about the subject of the poem.

Reflections

On the way home from school, try to find an object that is simple yet interesting. It might be a leaf or flower of exquisite shape or colour, an old candy wrapper, or an unusual pattern in the buildings around you. Whatever the object, it will take some imagination to find the extraordinary in the ordinary. If possible, bring the object, or a picture of it, to class.

Study the object and make notes about its uniqueness, the impressions it left on you, and how it captivated your senses.

Convert your ideas into a **free-verse** poem about the object. Keep in mind the following revision strategies:

- Organize your ideas into lines of poetry of one word to several words in length.
- Eliminate unnecessary words.
- Sharpen your **images** with figures of speech.
- Use only present-tense verbs.
- Consult a thesaurus to find descriptive words and phrases.
- Consider repeating certain words and phrases to emphasize your ideas.

SHARING AND PUBLISHING

W E A R A B L E   A R T

Using fabric paints or markers, reproduce your "reflections" poem on a piece of clothing. Add illustrations which complement the images in your poem. If your school has a Practical Arts lab, experiment with silk-screening your poem on a t-shirt or sweatshirt.

Reflections

Social Issues

every day, news reports are filled with problems facing your community, your country, and people in other parts of the world. Although many of these social problems may seem remote from your life, each one directly or indirectly affects you. What can you do about them? Sometimes the answer seems to be "nothing," and that can be very frustrating. But, if you learn more about these problems and develop an informed opinion, you may be able to have an impact on them. You can also express your views about social issues in many ways, by speaking and writing about your feelings.

The poets featured in this unit comment on social issues of importance to them: racism, child abuse, poverty, political oppression, Aboriginal land rights, and others. If you have opinions about these or other issues, try expressing your ideas in the form of poetry. There is no guarantee that writing about a social issue will solve it, but if no one makes an effort to correct the problems society faces, these problems will continue to exist.

The spirit of truth and the spirit of freedom — they are the pillars of society.
— Henrik Ibsen

Victor Jara

by **Alexandra Varela** (student)

That which meant more to him
    than the world—
    Even more than life itself—
they took from him

and left the two stumps
    of his broken dreams,
two gaping wounds never to be healed
by the passage of time—
    only by death.

My people,
today I feel your sorrow
    like a knife in my heart.
The tears of thousands wet my eyes.

Why has it taken me so long to realize?
The only thing that I can do,
    that I must do,
is give you back your hands,
so that his memory will live forever
in the minds and hearts of those
freed from the living death
    you now endure so bitterly.

In the little world in which children have their existence, . . . there is nothing so finely perceived and so finely felt, as injust[o]

— Charles Dickens

The Child Who Walks Backwards

by *Lorna Crozier*

My next-door neighbour tells me
her child runs into things.
Cupboard corners and doorknobs
have pounded their shapes
into his face. She says
he is bothered by dreams,
rises in sleep from his bed
to steal through the halls
and plummet like a wounded bird
down the flight of stairs.

This child who climbed my maple
with the sureness of a cat,
trips in his room, cracks
his skull on the bedpost,
smacks his cheeks on the floor.
When I ask about the burns
on the back of his knee,
his mother tells me
he walks backwards
into fireplace grates
or sits and stares at flames
while sparks burn stars in his skin.

Other children write their names
on the casts that hold
his small bones.
His mother tells me
he runs into things,
walks backwards,
breaks his leg
while she lies
sleeping.

In Remembrance

(For Uncle Minoru, Died January, 1984)　　　　　*by **Janice Mirikitani***

We gather at your coffin,
Uncle Minoru.
Mother, with her hands like gardenias
touches your sleeves.
We whisper of how well you look
peaceful in your utter silence.
How much we remember.
Why now, at death?
　　　Your kindnesses, Uncle,
as you crafted paper monkeys,
multicolored birds
to climb and jerk on a stick
to amuse children who gathered
at your innocent dark eyes,
always slightly moist.
We would jump on your back, riding you
like a silent horse,
as you lumbered on your hands and knees
from room to room.
　　　How much we remember…
we rode your shoulders,
knotted with hurt,
dressed in faded denim, smelling like
laundry soap and fish.
You never complained of it
only through those dark moist eyes.
And your smile
that drew living animals to you,
even wild birds.
Obachan said they could smell
the wounds hiding in your throat,

Social Issues

the wound in your heart
pierced by unjust punishment, racism, and rejection
sharp as blades.

      When did you vow silence, Minoru?
After the camps,
after you buried a daughter?
You slumped into a light
of your own and let life ride you.
Your daughter thrown broken
on the road by a drunk driver
who mumbled she flew from nowhere like a dumb chicken,
stretched out $200, not one apology
and said we were safer in the camps.

      Was there nothing left to say, Minoru,
as you slapped away his hot white hand?

      How much we remember…
When they took you to Amache Gate
locked us up like herded horses,
your dark innocent eyes, moist
with disbelief at charges of
sabotage, espionage,
your shoulders staggered from the lies.
Fear like a cold finger
pressed at your heart.
Life gasped like a beached fish.
The sky scummed over with clouds
and punishment without crime
stabbed between the blades of your back.

      Was there nothing left to say?
Minoru, the children who rode you
have tongues like birds.
We chatter. We remember
the mounds of hurt at your shoulders.
Could we but massage them to soothe
the pain, but death

makes our regrets scattered as apologies.
We did not expect them
to rip the coat of pride from your bones
nor the melody from your throat.
　　　Yes, there is much to say.
We will not leave your memory
as a silent rancid rose.
Our tongues become livid with history and
demands for reparations.
Crimes are revealed like the bloody lashes
of a fallen whip:
　　　the falsehoods, deletions, the conspiracy
　　　to legalize mass imprisonment.
No, we will not forget
　　　Amache Gate, Rohwer, Poston, Heart Mountain,
　　　Minidoka, Jerome, Gila River, Manzanar,
　　　Topaz, Tule Lake.
Our tongues are sharp like blades,
we overturn furrows of secrecy.
　　　Yes, we will harvest justice.
And Uncle, perhaps
your spirit will return
alive in a horse, or a bird,
riding free in the wind,
life surging through
the sinews of your strong shoulders.
　　　And yes,
the struggle continues on
with our stampede of voices.

Waterpot

*by **Grace Nichols***

The daily going out
and coming in
always being hurried
along
like like…cattle

In the evenings
returning from the fields
she tried hard to walk
like a woman

she tried very hard
pulling herself erect
with every three or four
steps
pulling herself together
holding herself like
royal cane

And the overseer
hurrying them along
in the quickening darkness

And the overseer sneering
them along in the quickening
darkness
sneered at the pathetic
the pathetic display
of dignity

O but look
there's a waterpot growing
from her head

Yuh Hear 'Bout?

*by **Valerie Bloom***

Yuh hear bout di people dem arres
Fi bun dung di Asian people dem house?
Yuh hear bout di policeman dem lock up
Fi beat up di black bwoy widout a cause?
Yuh hear bout di MP dem sack because im
     refuse fi help
Im coloured constituents in a dem fight
     'gainst deportation?
Yuh no hear bout dem?
Me neida.

Then

*by **Robert Hilles***

poverty teaches no one
it's just dark and small
like a revolver
always ready to be
the final judge.

i remember dirty walls
macaroni, television and
dumping the slop pail.
there was no beauty
you just survived
between paydays.

my father
drank every friday
and saturday nights.
he lived between the
borders of the day shift
and the night shift.
that was the only
structure i knew.

i know now
that he sold
what little of himself
he had so that i could eat.
what kind of change is that?

where one generation sacrifices
itself so that the next one
can walk on its bones
with a new pair of shoes.

Elephants

Patrick Lane

The cracked cedar bunkhouse
hangs behind me like a grey pueblo
in the sundown where I sit
to carve an elephant
from a hunk of brown soap
for the Indian boy who lives
in the village a mile back
in the bush.

The alcoholic truck-driver
and the cat-skinner sit beside me
with their eyes closed
all of us waiting out the last hour
until we go back on the grade

and I try to forget the forever
clank   clank   clank
across the grade
pounding stones and earth to powder
for hours in mosquito darkness
of the endless cold mountain night.

The elephant takes form—
my knife caresses smooth soap
scaling off curls of brown
which the boy saves to take home
to his mother in the village

Finished, I hand the carving to him
and he looks at the image of the great
beast for a long time
then sets it on dry cedar
and looks up at me:

                What's an elephant?
he asks
so I tell him of the elephants
and their jungles. The story
of the elephant graveyard
which no one has ever found
and how the silent
animals of the rain forest
go away to die somewhere
in the limberlost of distances
and he smiles

tells me of his father's
graveyard where his people have been
buried for years. So far back
no one remembers when it started
and I ask him where the graveyard is
and he tells me it is gone
now where no one will ever find it
buried under the grade of the new
highway.

Sometimes When It Rains

by *Geina Mhlope*

Sometimes when it rains
I smile to myself
And think of times when as a child
I'd sit by myself
And wonder why people need clothes

Sometimes when it rains
I think of times
when I'd run into the rain
Shouting 'Nkce—nkce mlanjana
When will I grow?
I'll grow up tomorrow!'

Sometimes when it rains
I think of times
When I watched goats
running so fast from the rain
While sheep seemed to enjoy it

Sometimes when it rains
I think of times
When we had to undress
Carry the small bundles of uniforms and books
On our heads
And cross the river after school

Sometimes when it rains
I remember times
When it would rain hard for hours
And fill our drum
so we didn't have to fetch water
From the river for a day or two
Sometimes when it rains

Rains for many hours without break
I think of people
who have nowhere to go
No home of their own
And no food to eat
Only rain water to drink

Sometimes when it rains
Rains for days without break
I think of mothers
Who give birth in squatter camps
Under plastic shelters
At the mercy of cold angry winds

Sometimes when it rains
I think of "illegal" job seekers
in big cities
Dodging police vans in the rain
Hoping for darkness to come
So they can find some wet corner to hide in

Sometimes when it rains
Rains so hard hail joins in
I think of life prisoners
in all the jails of the world
And wonder if they still love
To see the rainbow at the end of the rain

Sometimes when it rains
With hail stones biting the grass
I can't help thinking they look like teeth
Many teeth of smiling friends
Then I wish that everyone else
Had something to smile about.

Poet

(for Irina Ratushinskaya)   *by **Vikram Seth***

She lived for six years in a cage. When I
Am inclined to regret the way things are, I think
Of her who through long cold and pain did not
Betray the ones she loved or plead for mercy.
They censored the few letters they allowed.
Cabbage and bread, rotten and stale, were food.
While outside governments and springs went round
And summits, thaws, and great events occurred,
Here inside was no hope. Years of her youth
Were sickened for no crime. She did not even
Know if her lover knew she was alive.
The paper she'd written poems on was removed.
What could she find? — the swirls in the cold blue light
Through bars so thick her hands could not pass through them —
Those swirls of blue light and the heels of bread
She shared with some companionable mouse.
Her poems she memorized line by line and destroyed.
The Contents were what was difficult to remember.

I shall

*by **Fouzi El-Asmar***

  I shall create
out of the darkness of my jail
my dawn
out of the jaws of hatred
my destiny.
I shall sing
the wind
the sun
the flowers
the spring.
I shall sing
in spite of fences
in spite of jailers
in spite of hatred.

PERSONAL PERSPECTIVE

Hold a small-group discussion about the issues featured in the poems in this unit. Choose a social issue which is of particular concern to you (either one of the issues in the poems, or an issue of your choice). Make notes about why you chose this issue, what you know about it, and what you might do to solve some of the problems associated with it. Consult newspaper and magazine articles for further information and ideas. Write a poem in the form of a journal entry outlining your thoughts, feelings, and solutions to the problem. You may find the following steps useful in organizing your ideas:

- Write down the social issue and identify what initially drew your attention to the topic.
- Explore several solutions to the problem, then choose the best one.
- Summarize the whole issue and end your poem with a personal statement.
- Ensure your thoughts and ideas are conveyed using the first person.
- Add an appropriate title.

Edit and proofread your poem, then share it with several of your classmates. You may want to compare your perspective on the issue with classmates who chose the same topic.

WRITING FOCUS

SOCIAL COMMENTARY

Gather newspapers and collect headlines that could be used as lines (or partial lines) in a **found poem** dealing with an important social issue. You can gather these headlines randomly, or with some thematic purpose; for example, you may want your poem to make a statement about a certain topic. Choose headlines from a combination of categories:

accident reports, police reports, movie reviews, news broadcasts, sports reports. Juggle your headlines and add comments or lines of your own until you feel you have made your social comment in a poetic manner.

S O N G   L Y R I C S

Some poems in this unit refer to individuals who do not have the freedom to speak their mind. Discuss the following questions as a class: Why is the concept of freedom of speech so important to Canada's democratic society? Why do you think some societies suppress the voices of the people? What other methods do people use to communicate their ideas and opinions?

In ancient cultures, people devised chants and songs to communicate information about people, events, and phenomena. What are some of the issues facing your community and country today that could be shared in the form of a song. Choose one social issue that you feel is particularly important, and compose lyrics to a song about your topic. If you have access to musical instruments and/or recording equipment, prepare an audiotape of your song to share with the class.

SHARING AND PUBLISHING

Thematic Poster
Create a poster organized around a social issue featured in one of your poems. Incorporate pictures from newspapers and magazines, as well as a copy of your poem, into your poster.

Publish It
Submit the final draft of one of your social issues poems to your school or community newspaper for publication consideration.

The Threatened Environment

People today are becoming increasingly concerned with the preservation of their natural world. Our population has tripled since the beginning of the century and this increase in numbers is threatening the planet. Today, on every continent, humans are occupying and adapting more and more land to meet the demands of expanding populations for food and goods. As a result, the last great wilderness areas of the earth—the Amazon jungles, the Northern tundra, the forests of New Guinea—are being destroyed. Some facts to consider:

- The average North American produces approximately 590 kilograms of trash per year.
- Millions of fish, mammals, turtles, and birds are killed by the approximately six and a half billion kilograms of garbage that is dumped into the oceans every year.
- Experts estimate that plastic refuse kills more than 100 000 sea mammals and two million seabirds annually.
- Plastic six-pack rings take 450 years to degrade; the rings are commonly found around the necks of wildlife.
- Currently, only five percent of tin cans are recycled.

The good news is that worldwide awareness of the problems threatening our environment is increasing. What to do about these problems is the crucial question we now face. Some of the attempts being made to improve the present environmental situation include the following:

- Biological controls: the use of natural processes to achieve a desired result.
- Conservation: caring for wild animals and their natural habitats. Wildlife conservation laws are being more strictly enforced.
- Saving habitat: more protected areas are being established.
- Organizations: such as the International Union for Conservation of Nature are being formed to help conserve the environment.
- Legislation: many nations have passed laws to protect wildlife and the environment.
- Captive breeding: raising animals in captivity where they are provided with necessary resources and protection from harm.

While some problems cannot be overcome by individual action, many can. As individuals change their lifestyle, cultures are transformed. Lifestyles, however, only change when attitudes change, and attitudes only change through persuasion. The following poems are the poets' way of trying to express their beliefs and change the attitudes of others.

The Rhino

by *Kirsty Butcher* (student)

The rhino is a child's model
made out of clay,
the crinkly folds casting shadows
over its rainy day back.
Its big sad eyes stare at you
as if to say, "Help me."
His creased eyelids blink
back the tears.

His legs — stubbed out cigarette ends,
wallow in the mud, making craters
in the soil.
The horn — a huge cornet
of matted hair —
is the jinx of the rhino.
That is all he is hunted for.
And the lead from the bullets
has turned his skin grey.

Bison

by *Tonye Garter* (student)

Where has he gone?
The great shaggy beast.
The wild one.
The provider,
The warmth from cold.
The food to drive away hunger.
The robe and moccasins for my feet.
The leather for my shirt.
The skin for my tent.
The bones for my tools.
The sinew for my bowstring.
The horn for my spoon and cups.
The stomach for a bag to carry my things in.
The rawhide.
I look for him on the plains and he is not there.
I look for him in the meadows and the valleys
        and at the water and
he is not there either.
I cannot live without him.

If the beasts were gone, men would die from great loneliness of spirit.

— **Chief Seattle**

The Passenger Pigeon

*by **Paul Fleischman***

We were counted not in

        thousands

nor

        millions

but in
billions.

        billions.
        We were numerous as the

stars

        stars
        in the heavens

As grains of
sand
at the sea

        sand

        As the
buffalo
        buffalo
        on the plains.

When we burst into flight

        we so filled the sky

that the
sun
        sun
was darkened

        and
day
        day
        became dusk.

Humblers of the sun
        Humblers of the sun
we were!
        we were!
The world
inconceivable
        inconceivable
        without us.

Yet it's 1914,
and here I am
alone
        alone
        caged in the Cincinnati Zoo.

the last

        of the passenger pigeons.

Lynx In Winnipeg

*by **W.D. Valgardson***

His stiff fur
Bristles. He looks neither to left
Nor right. His feet
Scuff dust dropped from chimneys.
Over the years, his forests have grown houses.
Unable to tell what
Is his, he has come to reclaim it,
To see if boards will remember how to sprout branches.
In an hour his daily dream of rabbits
Will be lost in the white snarl of dogs
As he crouches in a tree without leaves.
A bullet will open his chest,
Releasing ten thousand memories of frogs
On the soft edges of streams, snow turning purple
With night, warm blood after a long hunt.
All this will be lost.
At the last, he will draw back, his yellow coat
As hard as quills, his mouth
Defiant, his claws rending the air.
His body will back itself into the distance
As though he would climb for heaven or a new world
Of tree tops and blue sky. His death will not come
Easily. Out of his place, he will drive
Others out of their lives until
A young man with a wife and two children
To whom he is kind, will ease himself
From his car, raise his heavy rifle,
Nestle wood to cheek.
Hedges are forests grown impotent.

So Many Forests

by *Jacques Prévert*
(translated by Kenneth F. Canfield)

So many forests torn out of the earth
and massacred
done in
rolled flat

So many forests sacrificed for paper pulp
billions of newspapers drawing annually
the attention of readers to the denudation
of the woods and forests.

In My World

by *Steve Turner*

In my world
I would write
of golden suns
if it weren't
for the obscuring clouds.
I would write
of the wind-bent grass
but all the fields
are tarmacked
& multistorey.
Instead I'll be
an urban Wordsworth
writing of
reinforced concrete landscapes
& clearbrown skies
where
to wander lonely as a cloud
is just not advisable
after dark.

A Green Prayer

*by **Jane Whittle***

Save me a clean stream, flowing
to unpolluted seas;

lend me the bare earth, growing
untamed flowers and trees.

May I share safe skies
when I wake, every day,

with birds and butterflies?
Grant me a space where I can play

with water, rocks, trees and sand;
lend me forests, rivers, hills and sea.

Keep me a place in this old land,
somewhere to grow, somewhere to be.

For Better or For Worse®   **by Lynn Johnston**

WRITING FOCUS

E N V I R O N M E N T A L   C O N C E R N

In a small group, read aloud an article that deals with the destruction of an ecological balance or a threat to our environment. You might find your particular interest lies in one of the following areas:

- polluted beaches and forests
- endangered species
- vanishing wilderness
- disappearing tropical rainforests
- acid rain
- oil spills
- the greenhouse effect

Discuss how the natural environment is managed in your community, and what you as a citizen are personally doing to care for the environment. What else could you do to help improve the quality of the environment in your particular geographical area?

Based on the discussion, write a poem that expresses your feelings about one specific environmental concern. Organize your poem using the following steps as a guideline:

a) Set the scene by establishing the problem.
b) Describe one encounter you personally have had with the problem.
c) Summarize your thoughts in the form of a personal statement.

WRITING FOCUS

E N D A N G E R E D   S P E C I E S

As humans, do we have a responsibility to ensure the well-being of the animals on the planet, to protect rather than exploit them? Do all animals have the right to life, to humane treatment, and to experience the intrinsic nature of their species?

Work in a small group and discuss your opinions about wildlife conservation. You may wish to comment on the following aspects of wildlife management:

- Is wildlife in danger?
- How might you assist with wildlife conservation?
- What are your thoughts concerning the fur industry?
- Should hunting and shooting animals for sport be allowed?
- How do you feel about the use of animals in medical research?

Working on your own, pretend you are an animal whose species is in danger. Write a poem in role as the animal outlining your experiences and fears. Avoid including the name of the animal in your poem. To help you focus your thoughts, describe the animal, consider the expression on the animal's face and where the animal is—in the jungle, at the zoo, or in some other location.

Read the final draft of your poem to your group members and have them guess what animal you have written about. Consider offering clues using miming techniques.

WRITING FOCUS

PICTURE PERFECT

Look for intriguing photos from magazines and newspapers that show some aspect of environmental destruction and/or conservation, such as: the slaughtering of animals, anti-fur activists, over-fishing, the efforts of the World Wildlife Fund or Greenpeace, littering, air pollution, logging, insecticides, acid rain.

Bring your photos to class and makes notes on what is particularly interesting about each one. What, if any, type of conflict do the photos document? What might happen next? Choose one of the photos and, based on your notes, write a poem that might accompany the action in the picture. Your poem should include your emotional response to the photo.

Poetic Protest

Compile a booklet of poems written by your classmates and send it to an appropriate governmental agency, politician, community newspaper, or local radio station.

Wildlife Poster

Read one of your "wildlife" poems to a group of younger students and collaborate with them to design a poster about wildlife preservation. Use any artistic medium you wish. Your **theme** might be "Helping Wildlife Together."

> **COMPUTER TIP**
>
> If you plan to publish a collection of your poetry, include a title for your collection along with a page number on each page by using the "header" or "footer" function of your computer program.

Recycled Rainforest

As a class, create a rainforest using recycled objects and hang your environment poems from the "branches."

Destroyed buildings can be rebuilt, and destroyed works of art may possibly be replaced by new creations. But every animal and every flower which becomes extinct is lost forever in the most absolute of deaths.

— Joseph Wood Krutch

The Threatened Environment

Technically Speaking

Spectacular is a word that describes the past thirty years of development in the field of technology. The importance of technology in our world, in our daily lives, is enormous. Can you imagine what life would be like without electricity, without combustion engines to power our cars, without clocks, telephones, computers, and televisions? Would you be willing to give up all of your technological devices? Probably not…and with good reason. We like what technology does for us. It allows us to solve problems and accomplish goals. Amazing advances in science and technology have enabled humankind to escape disease, overpopulation, pollution, and other problems.

The benefits of these technologies, however, come with a price. A great many of our fears and frustrations are bound up with the ominous power of the technology we have created. Technology threatens our freedom, it often makes our lives complicated, it is difficult to control, and, above all, it has the awesome power to destroy life.

The technological advances of the next few decades are likely to bring about the most striking changes in our quality of life. You are part of the "high-tech" world of tomorrow. It is the world you and your children will live in. If we use our new discoveries wisely and plan ahead thoughtfully, that world should be an exciting place.

Computer, Computer

*by **Wendy Shewfelt** (student)*

SEARCH out a love.
i am but a #
lost
in PRINT-OUTS of
lonely figures
10's and 0's,
personified digits without heroes.

COMPUTER, supposed
saviour of this day
RUN...
the solution
to our hunger and dismay.
comfort the victims
in this technological race,
and, don't forget to
POWER OFF, if
you aim
to maintain
face.

Our lives are changed by the vision— and persistence—of individuals willing to pursue new ideas.

— P. Ranganath Nayak and John Ketteringham

The Computer

by **Raymond Souster**

So much of our lives now
entrusted to its care.
What if suddenly
it should fail us?

It must have guessed our concern,
for it instantly replies:
have no fear,
I'm all-powerful,
with none of the failings
of you humans,
nothing possibly
can or will go wrong.

Which is unfortunate.
If it hadn't said anything
we might have buried our doubts
and believed in it.

Mad Ad

by **Roger McGough**

A Madison Avenue whizzkid
thought it a disgrace
That no one had exploited
the possibilities in space
Discussed it with a client
who agreed and very soon
A thousand miles of neontubing
were transported to the moon.

Now no one can ignore it
the product's selling fine
The night they turned the moon
into a Coca-Cola sign.

pity this busy monster, manunkind

by e.e. cummings

pity this busy monster, manunkind,

not. Progress is a comfortable disease:
your victim (death and life safely beyond)

plays with the bigness of his littleness
— electrons deify one razorblade
into a mountainrange; lenses extend

unwish through curving wherewhen till unwish
returns on its unself.
                    A world of made
is not a world of born — pity poor flesh

and trees, poor stars and stones, but never this
fine specimen of hypermagical

ultraomnipotence. We doctors know

a hopeless case if — listen: there's a hell
of a good universe next door; let's go

20th Century

by Louis Dudek

And to protect the consumer
manufacturers were required
to state the main ingredients
on the label, e.g. —

"Di-isobutyl-phenoxy-ethoxy-
    ethyl-dimethyl-benzyl-
    ammonium-chloride"

by way of guidance and assistance to the buyer.

▶ I'm Sorry Says the Machine

*by **Eve Merriam***

I'm sorry says the machine,
Thank you for waiting says the tape recording,
Trying to connect you says the voice in the
    vacuum at the end of the line.

I'm sorry that sister is not in working order.
Please verify your brother and try him again.
I'm sorry that mother is out of service.
Thank you for waiting, that father you have
    reached is a temporary disconnect.

I'm sorry that landlord is not in working order.
Please verify your neighborhood and try it again.
I'm sorry those repairs are out of service.
Thank you for waiting, that official you have
    reached is not reachable at this time.

I'm sorry that water is not in drinking order.
Please verify that sunlight and try it later.
I'm sorry that blue sky is out of service.
Thank you for waiting, those flowers and trees
    are permanently disconnected.

I'm sorry that country is not in working order.
I'm sorry that planet is out of service.
Please verify that godhead and try much later.
Thank you for waiting, that universe has been
    dis—.

*Our heads are round so that our
thinking can change direction.*
— Francis Picabia

Cool Medium

*by **David Sutton***

In fifty-three the children up our road
Got television and disappeared indoors
After school, instead of coming out
To toast crusts over stick fires in the hedgerow
Or fill the first-starred, batwinged dusks of autumn
With clamour of wild games. I sulked around

The silent woods, refused their invitations,
And hated ever since those moon-grey flickers
From a dead planet. Now, at night, I still
Walk past curtained windows, knowing each
Conceals that strange communion. Is life
Something to be given up for that?

Amused, superior, grown-up faces smile:
The awkward child stalks in the woodland still,
Keeping the ward of long-abandoned places,
As if one day the others might come back,
Stubborn in an antique heresy,
With trees and winter stars for company.

© 1976 by Chicago Tribune
N.Y. News Synd. Inc.

In a small group, discuss whether technological inventions free up our time or enslave us further. Take into consideration the ethics of computer use in society. For example, factory assembly-line workers are losing their jobs to robot workers.

Individually, choose what you feel to be the most beneficial and the most destructive technological invention and **juxtapose** the two in a poem. Or, select any technological invention and discuss its influence in the form of a **free-verse** poem. You may want to research one or more of the following innovative technologies before you begin writing your poem:

- the information superhighway
- advanced computer software
- digital television
- virtual reality
- voice-controlled appliances
- electric cars
- smart-house features
- sophisticated car audio systems
- flat-screen televisions
- computerized home management systems to monitor security, lights, appliances, and the environment
- new video games
- high-resolution televisions
- electronic library programs
- electronic wall painting
- state-of-the-art home videos
- robotics
- supercomputer graphics

... Poetry —
all of it —
is a journey to the unknown.
— Vladimir Mayakovski

G A D G E T   G O T C H A !

W rite a humorous poem about some frustrating experience (either real or imagined) that you have had with some "gadget." You might consider the latest in televisions, telephones, computers, interactive electronics, camping equipment, musical instruments, and household appliances. You may want to include a warning to future users about some of the pitfalls, or discuss your experiences with your "robot home-helper."

I N V E N T O R /   I N V E N T I O N

R esearch the development of some major technological invention which is pervasive in our society, such as the computer or the television. Then, write a poem from the perspective of the inventor, outlining his or her trials and tribulations during the creative process.

Or, pretend you *are* the invention. Imagine, for example, that you are a robot who has been programmed to have human feelings but your owners do not know that. Describe your many emotions in the form of a short poem or song lyrics. What are your problems? Are you lonely or sad as the only robot in the house? Think about other robots, droids, cyborgs, androids, and so on, that you have seen in movies. Perhaps they will inspire you as you formulate your thoughts in role.

SHARING AND PUBLISHING

I nvent a new product that would solve a particular problem and create an ad campaign for it. Your poem could become an advertising jingle which you could audio- or videotape.

Technically Speaking

Looking Out

because our world changes with breathtaking speed, it is important for us to look ahead and prepare ourselves for the future. Even now, you may be wondering and dreaming about your future. If so, you are among those people who believe there is not one future but many futures; futures that are possible, probable, and preferable. Future-oriented people believe that today's choices dictate tomorrow's reality. They focus on the period five to twenty years ahead and are pro-active (not reactive) toward the future.

The basic foundation for predicting the future is observation. Watching the development of emerging trends will give you some indication of what to expect in the coming years. As the following list of trends and ideas suggests, we are in for a whirlwind of change.

- artificial moons
- 3D photography
- superperformance fabrics
- genetic control
- sea farming
- living at sea/undersea
- longer life
- automated shopping
- lasers and masers
- space travel improvements
- battery operated television
- synthetic foods
- space living systems
- human hibernation
- programmed dreams
- conference television

The world is changing so fast and technology is advancing so rapidly that your life will probably be very different from what you imagine today. The important thing to remember is that the future doesn't have to be something that just happens to you. As you are "looking out" to the future, ask yourself the question, "What is the best possible future world I can imagine...and how do I get there from here?"

To Dream

*by **Michelle Blough** (student)*

I like to dream
Of how the world could be,
Of how I'd like the world to be.
I like to dream
Of how my life could be,
Of how I'd like my life to be.

I like to dream
Of unending things
Like sunsets,
    For there is always another;
Like merry-go-rounds,
    For they never stop;
Like rainbows,
    For they never end;
Like unicorns,
    For they will always live;
Like tears,
    For there are always more to fall.

I like to dream
Of freedom in the world.
Of how I'd like to be free
Like birds in the sky,
    Able to see the world
    From on high;
Like true friends,
    Letting you be
    Just who you want to be;
Like comets in the night,
    Living for eternity,
    Just to shine again and again.

I like to dream
Of how the world could be,
Of how I'd like the world to be.

My interest is in the future because I'm going to spend the rest of my life there.

— Charles F. Kettering

Youth

by **Langston Hughes**

We have tomorrow
Bright before us
Like a flame.

Yesterday
A night-gone thing,
A sun-down name.

And dawn-today
Broad arch above the road we came.

We march!

The Road Not Taken

by **Robert Frost**

Two roads diverged in a yellow wood,
And sorry I could not travel both
And be one traveller, long I stood
And looked down one as far as I could
To where it bent in the undergrowth;

Then took the other, as just as fair,
And having perhaps the better claim,
Because it was grassy and wanted wear;
Though as for that the passing there
Had worn them really about the same,

And both that morning equally lay
In leaves no step had trodden black.
Oh, I kept the first for another day!
Yet knowing how way leads on to way,
I doubted if I should ever come back.

I shall be telling this with a sigh
Somewhere ages and ages hence:
Two roads diverged in a wood, and I—
I took the one less travelled by,
And that has made all the difference.

dreamer

*by **Jean 'Binta' Breeze***

roun a rocky corner
by de sea
seat up
    pon a drif wood
yuh can fine she
gazin cross de water
a stick
    eena her han
trying to trace
      a future
   in de san

Change is the law of life, and those who look only to the past or present are certain to miss the future.

— John F. Kennedy

Looking Out

The Door

by **Miroslav Holub**
(translated by Ian Milner and George Theiner)

Go and open the door.
    Maybe outside there's
    a tree, or a wood,
    a garden,
    or a magic city.

Go and open the door.
    Maybe a dog's rummaging.
    Maybe you'll see a face,
or an eye,
or the picture

            of a picture.

Go and open the door.
    If there's a fog
    it will clear.

Go and open the door.
Even if there's only
    the darkness ticking,
    even if there's only
    the hollow wind,
    even if
        nothing
           is there,
go and open the door.

At least
there'll be
a draught.

*It takes only one person
to change your life—you.*
— Ruth Casey

Highway 16/5 Illumination

*by **Tom Wayman***

South-east of Edmonton, on the road that leads
to Vermilion, Lloydminster, and the Saskatchewan border
I feel coming into me again like
a song about a man born in the country
the joy of the highway: the long road

that reaches ahead through these wooded rises, the farms
that spread their fields out around themselves
flat to the sun, the odor of hay filling the cabin of the car

mile by mile, border after border, horizon
to horizon. The highway stretches away
in all directions, linking and connecting
across an entire continent

and anywhere I point the front wheels
I can go.

WRITING FOCUS

BIOGRAPHICAL SKETCH

Invite a guidance or career counsellor to your class to answer questions about any career goals you and your classmates may have. You might list all the different steps you need to take in order to achieve your career and life goals.

Pretend it is your twenty-fifth high school reunion. You are in charge of making a booklet of biographical sketches that reveals what each person has been doing since he or she graduated. Choose one of your classmates (you may choose yourself). Write an imaginary biography that describes this person's life and occupation, and where she or he lives and works. Convert this biographical information into a poem. Read the following guidelines before beginning your poem:

- The ideas and/or feelings in a **lyric** or **free-verse** poem are much more important than the story.

Looking Out

- Use language imaginatively (careful word choice, effective use of figures of speech, skillful use of **diction** and sound devices).
- Communicate your ideas and emotion using as few words as possible.
- Do not write a biographical poem that would upset the person it is about.

WRITING FOCUS

FUTURE PREDICTIONS

A trend is the general direction in which things are going. Futurists examine trends and predict what will happen next. In a small group, discuss some of the items listed in the introduction on page 233 and indicate whether they represent actual trends. After discussing each item, formulate a prediction of your own. Explain your rationale for making this prediction and try to convince your group members that it is possible. Once you have addressed all their arguments, write a poem about your prediction.

WRITING FOCUS

LOOKING AHEAD

Consider your personal future. Imagine what your home, family, and leisure time might be like. What kind of a person would you like to be?

We all have wishes and dreams. Discuss this aspect of human nature with a partner, and jot down some of your wishes, plans, and dreams. You might think of answering questions such as the following:

- What are the strengths that I would like to have?
- What three wishes would I like to have come true?
- If I could have one gift or talent, what would it be?
- Which people from history would I like to meet?
- Who else would I like to meet?
- What fantastic thing would I like to do?

- What one thing would I like to do to benefit humankind?
- What kind of occupation would I like to have?
- What kind of training and education will I need?
- What do I think will be the most exciting thing about the future?

Working on your own, try to transform your ideas into the rough draft of a free-verse poem. Revise your poem with the help of your original partner. Be sure your ideas are presented clearly, then examine the effectiveness of your wording and style.

SHARING AND PUBLISHING

Imagine we have established contact with life forms on a planet in a distant galaxy and have discovered a way to communicate with each other. Canada's Prime Minister has created a number of poetry/art contests. Throughout Canada, all students in your grade have been asked to enter the contest. Here are the rules:

Poetry Component
Explain earthlings to our new friends. Brainstorm a list of important events in human history and/or facts about human beings. Because of the distance separating us, your message has to be brief. You can only beam out three statements. Which three pieces of information would you choose and why? Shape these statements into a short poem or song lyric.

Art Component
Design a postage stamp marking our first communication with other life forms.

Present your final product to your classmates. After all the presentations are finished, collect the projects into a classroom booklet. Give the booklet a title.

> ### COMPUTER TIP
>
> If your computer has a "define styles" function, it provides an easy way to give all your poetry a consistent look for later publication. You can set up styles for your title, the body of your poem, and your name. This will reduce the time it takes you to format each new poem.

ALLITERATION   The intentional repetition of similar initial sounds in two or more words. Alliteration is meant to appeal to the sense of sound.

> He clasps the crag with crooked hands;
> Close to the sun in lonely lands,
>> — from "The Eagle" by Alfred, Lord Tennyson

ALLUSION   A reference, usually brief, to a famous person, event, or work. Usually the writer expects the reader to understand the reference. (Sometimes obscure or complex allusions are used.) The most common allusions are to literature, historical events, religious lore, or mythology.

> e.g., The Edmonton Oilers' defence is their Achilles' heel. (This is an allusion to the Greek god Achilles, whose only vulnerable spot was his heel.)

ASSONANCE   The intentional repetition of an internal vowel sound in stressed syllables.

> Weak as the reed—weak—feeble as my voice—
> Oh, oh, the pain, the pain of feebleness.
>> — from "The Fall of Hyperion" by John Keats

Compare with **consonance**.

ATMOSPHERE   Atmosphere refers to the overall effect of a literary work that is created by the mood, setting, description, and dialogue. For example, the first sentence of Edgar Allan Poe's story, "The Fall of the House of Usher," creates an atmosphere of mystery and gloom:

> During the whole of a dull, dark, and soundless day in the autumn of the year, when the clouds hung oppressively low in the heavens, I had been passing alone, on horseback, through a singularly dreary tract of country, and at length found myself, as the shades of evening drew on, within view of the melancholy House of Usher.

See also **mood**.

BALLAD   A narrative poem that tells a dramatic story composed in short stanzas and designed for singing or oral recitation. Many ballads have been passed down, by word of mouth, from one generation to the next. Often there is no record of the original author, and the music and even parts of the original story may have been lost. Typically, ballads deal with culturally universal themes such as adventure, love, conflict, and the supernatural. Many Old English ballads have strong rhyme and rhythm, often

241

with a refrain. The modern ballad, also called a "literary" or "art ballad," has an acknowledged author and some claim to literary distinction. Ballads are still being written today, usually as popular music.

*See also **narrative poem, refrain**.*

CACOPHONY   A mixture of harsh, discordant, unpleasant sounds which may be difficult to articulate. Cacophony is used to jar the reader to attention.

*Compare with **euphony**.*

CADENCE   The rhythmic flow, or sequence, of sounds in writing and speaking.

CALLIGRAM

*See **shape poem**.*

CINQUAIN   In poetry, the word *cinquain* can refer to any stanza of five lines. The term also refers to a specific type of short poem whose form was invented by an American poet, Adelaide Crapsey, who had studied Japanese haiku. For more information, see the chapter on cinquain in *Section 2: Form and Formula*.

CONCRETE POETRY   A form of poetry in which the physical arrangement of the letters, words, and lines of poetry helps to convey the meaning of the poem.

CONNOTATION   The suggested or implied meanings and mental associations related to a word or phrase. For example, a literal meaning of the word "gold" is "a precious metal," but "gold" is also associated with power, riches, and luxury—its connotative meanings.

*Compare with **denotation**.*

CONSONANCE   The repetition of internal consonant sounds or end consonant sounds in words. Note the repetition of the "n" sound in the following lines from "The Windhover" by Gerard Manley Hopkins:

> I caught this morning morning's minion, kingdom of daylight's
> dauphin, dapple-dawn-drawn Falcon, in his riding
> Of the rolling level underneath him steady air...

*Compare with **assonance**.*

COUPLET   A pair of successive lines of poetry, especially a pair that rhyme and have the same number of syllables. Each of William Shakespeare's sonnets concludes with a rhymed couplet.

> And yet, by heaven, I think my love as rare
> As any she belied with false compare.
>
>   — from "Sonnet 130" by William Shakespeare

DENOTATION   The literal, dictionary meaning of a word or phrase. Thus, the denotation of *fox* is "a carnivorous mammal of the genus *Vulpes*, related to the dogs and wolves, and characteristically having upright ears, a pointed snout, and a long, bushy tail." If the word, however, suggests to the listener or reader "a crafty, sly or clever person," it has acquired a connotation.

Compare with **connotation**.

DIAMANTE   A simple diamond-shaped poem that expresses contrast, invented by Iris McClellan Tiedt, an American writer, teacher, and librarian. The most common diamantes consist of seven lines with a distinct structure. For more information, see the chapter on diamante in *Section 2: Form and Formula*.

DICTION   Refers to an author's or a speaker's choice and use of words to convey meaning. In poetry, diction refers to the selection and arrangement of words in the poetic work. There are four levels of diction:

formal – used in formal speeches and in scholarly works
informal – the language used by most people
colloquial – terms and expressions characteristic of spoken language
slang – newly coined words and fad expressions

ELEGY   From Greek: *elegeia*, "lament." A poem with a mood of sorrow and regret. An elegy is often a lament for someone who has died. Among well-known elegies are Thomas Gray's "Elegy Written in a Country Churchyard" and Walt Whitman's "When Lilacs Last in the Dooryard Bloom'd."

EPIGRAM   A short, witty saying or poem, often but not always consisting of two rhyming lines. Hilaire Belloc, a well-known novelist, is known for this epigram:

> When I am dead,
> I hope it may be said,
> "His sins were scarlet,
> But his books were read."

EPITAPH   A brief poem or prose statement praising a dead person and usually inscribed on a tomb or gravestone. The following is John Gay's epitaph on his tomb in Westminster Abbey:

> Life is a jest and all things show it.
> I thought so once, and now I know it.

EUPHONY   From the Greek word meaning "sweet-voiced." The musical effect caused by a smooth combination of sounds which are pleasant to the ear. Euphony contains pleasant-sounding letters. Most well-written poems are euphonious.

> The moan of doves in immemorial elms
> And murmuring of innumerable bees,
> — from "Come Down, O Maid" by Alfred, Lord Tennyson

*Compare with **cacophony**.*

FIGURATIVE LANGUAGE   Writing or speech characterized by the use of simile, metaphor, personification, and other *figures of speech*. A writer uses figurative language mainly to compare seemingly dissimilar things and to clarify for the reader the images he or she is trying to present.

*See also **metaphor, oxymoron, personification, simile**.*

FOOT   A group of syllables making up a metrical unit in poetry, consisting of a set pattern of stressed and unstressed, or accented and unaccented, syllables. Different types of feet are labelled as follows:

anapest – two unstressed syllables followed by a stressed syllable
dactyl – a stressed syllable followed by two unstressed syllables
iamb – an unstressed syllable followed by a stressed syllable
spondee – two stressed syllables
trochee – a stressed syllable followed by an unstressed syllable

Poet Samuel Taylor Coleridge wrote the following lines in an attempt to illustrate metrical feet:

> Trochee/ trips from/ long to/ short;
>
> From long to long in solemn sort
>
> Slow Spon/dee stalks;/ strong foot!/ yet ill/ able
>
> Ever to/ come up with/ Dactyl tri/ syllable.
>
> Iam/bics march/ from short / to long;
>
> With a leap/ and a bound/ the swift An/apests throng.

*See also **metre**.*

FORM   In poetry, the metrical and stanzaic organization of a poem. The word "form" is used in many ways: verse form, stanza form, ballad form, elegy form, etc.

*See also **metre, stanza**.*

FOUND POETRY   Poetry is all around you. The images and rhythm of words often make statements poetic; e.g., "Red sky at night, is a sailor's delight." There are words in print all around you that are poetic, too. Sometimes the sound of the words, or their rhythm, or the way they have been laid out is striking. Found poetry is simply language which you have drawn from your environment and crafted into poetry. For more information, see the chapter on found poems in *Section 3: Shape and Style*.

FREE VERSE   Poetry that lacks a regular metrical pattern and line length, but instead tries to capture the rhythms of natural speech. It does not obey particular rules of spelling, line length, rhyme, or metre. Although most poetry written today is free verse, not everyone is in favour of this poetry form. For example, Robert Frost once commented, "Writing free verse is like playing tennis with the net down."

*See also **metre, rhyme**.*

HAIKU   A form of Japanese verse which, in its most traditional form, consists of 17 syllables: 5 in the first line, 7 in the second, and 5 in the third. A haiku is short and concise and usually deals with nature. For more information, see the chapter on haiku in the *Form and Formula* section.

HYPERBOLE   Obvious and deliberate exaggeration which may be either humorous or serious. For example: "I am dying for love."

IAMBIC PENTAMETER   A line of poetry containing five metrical feet, each of two syllables, the first stressed, the second unstressed. The following lines are written in iambic pentameter.

⌣ ‒ ⌣ ‒ ⌣ ‒ ⌣ ‒ ⌣ ‒
When I/ have fears/ that I/ may cease/ to be/
⌣ ‒ ⌣ ‒ ⌣ ‒ ⌣ ‒ ⌣ ‒
Before/ my pen/ has gleaned/ my teem/ ing brain/
— from "When I have fears" by John Keats

*See also **foot, metre**.*

IMAGE   A verbal representation of a person, object, or event. In poetry, an image refers to the impression left in a reader's mind by the poet's use of description. The image is a significant and necessary element of poetry.

IMAGERY   The use of language to appeal to one or more of the senses: taste, touch, sight, smell, or hearing. Most images are visual, but many poems appeal to senses other than sight. All the images in a poem taken together convey a particular mood.

*See also **mood**.*

IRONY   A statement in which the literal meaning is the opposite of the intended meaning, or a situation in which one's expectation of the outcome is reversed. In *Julius Caesar*, when Mark Antony says "Brutus is an honourable man," he means just the opposite, and the audience is aware of his true meaning, so the statement is ironic. In Jacques Prévert's poem "So Many Forests," it is ironic that trees are being cut down to make paper to print newspapers announcing the destruction of forests.

JUXTAPOSITION   The placing of things side by side for the sake of comparison. Often the elements have very little in common, creating a jarring effect on the reader.

LIGHT VERSE   Humorous poetry designed to entertain the reader. The limerick is a well-known form of light verse.

LYRIC   A type of poetry that presents a personal, often intense display of thoughts and emotions. Lyric is a widely used term, encompassing many different types of poetry.

METAPHOR   Poets often make surprising comparisons between things that do not seem to be connected at all. A direct comparison between two unlike objects is called a metaphor. Instead of using the words "like," "as," or "than," the way a simile does, a metaphor makes a comparison in a more subtle manner. Although metaphors are frequently used by poets, they are also common in everyday conversation. For example, if your parent says, "Your room is a garbage dump," that is a metaphor.

*Compare with **simile**.*

METRE   The rhythmical pattern created in most English poetry by a series of stressed and unstressed syllables. The basic metrical unit is the "foot."

*See also **foot, rhythm**.*

MONOLOGUE   In poetry, this term refers to a poem with the words of one person, who speaks to another person who is present but who does not respond. It originates in the Greek words meaning "one word" or "one speech."

MOOD   Mood is an element of atmosphere which refers to the feeling or emotional state that is created in the reader through the author's use of descriptive details. The word originates from the old English *mod* meaning "heart; courage."

See also **atmosphere**.

NARRATIVE POEM   A poem which tells either a fictional or a true story. "Narrative" is from a Latin word meaning "tell." A narrative poem may be a simple telling of an experience, a newspaper account of an event, or a complex plotted story. A *narrator* is the person who relates the story.

NONSENSE VERSE   A form of light verse, which is written to entertain. Although its structure may be formal, its subject and theme may be silly and absurd.

See also **light verse**.

ONOMATOPOEIA   The poetic use of words whose sounds seem to imitate the sounds associated with the action involved. For example, the word "splash" sounds like the noise made when something is thrown into water. Some other onomatopoeic words are slap, whisper, buzz, roar, growl, clang, crunch, screech.

OXYMORON   An expression which combines two apparently contradictory words to form a concise paradox, such as in the last two words in the following line from Shakespeare's *Romeo and Juliet*: "Parting is such *sweet sorrow*." Other examples include: "civil war," "guest host," "freezer burn," "plastic glasses."

PARADOX   A statement which appears to be self-contradictory, but contains an element of truth, as in the following statement from William Shakespeare's *Julius Caesar*: "Cowards die many times before their deaths."

PARODY   A comic or satirical imitation of a selection of writing by imitating or ridiculing its style and content.

PERSONA   The speaker or the "I" of a poem created by the poet. Although the poet's views may be very similar to those expressed in the poem, usually the poet is taking on a role and projecting his or her voice into an imagined character. "Persona" comes from the Latin word meaning "mask."

Glossary

247

PERSONIFICATION   A figure of speech in which nonhuman things, animals, and ideas are given human qualities. When writers write about leaves "dancing" or a lake "smiling," they are attributing human traits to nonhuman objects. The first stanza from "Who Am I?" by Felice Holman uses personification:

> The trees ask me,
> And the sky,
> And the sea asks me
> *Who am I?*

PICTURE POEM

See shape poem.

QUATRAIN   A stanza or poem of four lines. The quatrain is the most common stanzaic form in English verse.

See also stanza.

REFRAIN   Lines or part of a line repeated at intervals in a poem, often at the end of each stanza. These lines are used for a variety of reasons, such as emphasis, tone, or irony.

See also irony, stanza, tone.

RHYME   Similarity of sound in words. In rhyming poetry similar accented sounds are repeated, generally at the end of lines (*end rhyme*), but sometimes within lines (*internal rhyme*). A *rhyme scheme* is a pattern of rhyming lines in a poem. Letters of the alphabet are used to describe a rhyme scheme to show which lines rhyme with which other lines. For example, the first eight lines of a Petrarchan sonnet have the rhyme scheme *abbaabba*: the first, fourth, fifth, and eighth lines rhyme, and the second, third, sixth and seventh lines have a different rhyme.

See also sonnet.

RHYTHM   In poetry, rhythm refers to the patterns of accented and unaccented (stressed and unstressed) syllables. Rhythm is achieved through repetition. There are rhythms all around us: turn signals on a car, the waves crashing onto the shore, your heartbeat. Some rhythms are smooth and regular, others are jerky. Some rhythms are fast, some are slow.

SATIRE   Literature which blends criticism and humour, and holds up human vices and foibles to ridicule and scorn. Satire creates amusement in the reader in order to inspire correction of the faults being satirized.

SHAPE POEM   A shape poem, also called a *picture poem* or, more formally, a *calligram*, is a poem which takes the shape of its subject. Writers who produce calligrams are as interested in how words look as in how they sound. To appreciate a shape poem, it helps to put aside your usual ideas about language, and think about the poem as if it were a painting or a sculpture.

SIMILE   A figure of speech which makes a direct comparison between two unlike objects, using the words "like," "as," or "than." The following is a famous simile:

> She walks in beauty, like the night
> Of cloudless climes and starry skies;
> > — "She Walks in Beauty," by George Gordon, Lord Byron

SONNET   A poem of fourteen lines written in iambic pentameter with a specific *rhyme scheme*. The two principal sonnet forms are described below:

- *Petrarchan sonnet*: Also called an *Italian sonnet*, this type of sonnet was first popularized in Italy by Petrarch (1304-1374). It is divided into an *octave* (eight lines) and a *sestet* (six lines). The rhyme scheme is *abbaabba* for the octave, and *cdecde* or *cdedce* or *cdcdcd* or *cdccdc* for the sestet.
- *Shakespearean sonnet*: Also called an *English sonnet*, this sonnet form was first popularized in England by William Shakespeare (1564-1616). It is divided into three quatrains and a concluding rhyming couplet, usually with the rhyme scheme *abab cdcd efef gg*.

See also **couplet, iambic pentameter, quatrain, rhyme.**

STANZA

A group of two or more lines which make up a unit of a poem and contain a unity of thought and form. A poem may be divided into several stanzas. The stanzaic pattern of a poem is determined by the number of lines, the number of feet in each line, the metre, and the rhyme scheme.

See also **foot, metre, rhyme.**

SYMBOL   Something that stands for something else—an act, word, or tangible object that represents more than itself. Our country's flag, for example, symbolizes patriotism. Some symbols are "traditional," or common, in literature. For example, spring is a traditional symbol of life and rejuvenation, whereas autumn is a traditional symbol of decay and disintegration. Other symbols are "individual," or unique, to a particular selection of literature. *Symbolism* refers to all the symbols in a creative work taken together.

Glossary

TANKA   A form of Japanese verse which, in its most traditional form, consists of 31 syllables: 5 in the first line, 7 in the second, 5 in the third, 7 in the fourth, and 7 in the fifth. For more information, see the chapter on tanka in *Section 2: Form and Formula.*

THEME   The central or dominant idea that is present in any literary work. It may be a comment about life that the writer is trying to make.

TONE   The writer's attitude or point of view toward his or her subject and audience.

UNDERSTATEMENT   Understatement occurs when something is intentionally represented less strongly than the facts would call for. It is a form of irony. For example, if someone responds with the phrase, "That's nice" to the news that you have just won the lottery, she or he is using understatement.

* *(S)* = student poem

ALTERNATIVE THEMES

Alternative Themes

* *(S)* = student poem

CREDITS

Every reasonable effort has been made to find copyright holders for material contained in this book. The publishers gratefully acknowledge permission to reprint the following selections and would be pleased to correct any errors or omissions in future printings.

Poetry selections are arranged in alphabetical order by author surname. Cartoons are arranged in appearance order.

POETRY SELECTIONS

"The Last Shot" by Darryl J. Adamko reprinted by permission of the author. / "Diamante" is reprinted by permission of Lisa Nicole Anthony, Sydney, Nova Scotia. / "Creased," "Our Beautiful Society," and "Spiders" by Kelly Armstrong reprinted by permission of the author. / "Me As My Grandmother" by Rosemary Aubert, reprinted from *Two Kinds of Honey* by permission of Oberon Press. / "Mother's Arms" by Erin Baade. From *The Claremont Review*, Number Six, Fall 1994. Terence Young, Susan Stenson, and Bill Stenson, eds., Reprinted by permission of the author. / "Friends/Enemies" by Jonathan Bauer reprinted by permission of the author. / "Precious Bits of Family" by Linda Belarde. From *A Gathering of Spirits*, edited by Beth Brant. (Toronto: Women's Press, 1988; Ithaca: Firebrand, 1984) / "The Ichthyosaurus" by Isabel Frances Bellows appeared in *Oh, That's Ridiculous*, W. Cole, ed., The Viking Press, 1972. / "Siamese Fighting Fish" by Jason Benn reprinted by permission of Joseph I. Tsujimoto. / "Hockey" by Scott Blaine appeared in *Grab Me a Bus...and Other Award Winning Poems*, M. Glass and M.J. Eaton, eds., Scholastic Magazines, Inc., 1974. / "To Dream" by Michelle Blough reprinted by permission of the author. / "It's Raining in Love" by Richard Brautigan. From *The Pill versus the Springhill Mine Disaster* (copyright 1968). Reprinted by permission. / "dreamer" by Jean 'Binta' Breeze appeared in *Hearsay: Performance Poems Plus*, P. Beasley, ed., The Bodley Head, 1994. Originally appeared in *Riddym Ravings*, 1988. / "What Are Friends For" by Rosellen Brown appeared in *Perspectives Three*, E. Hannan *et al*, eds., Harcourt Brace Jovanovich, 1992. / "Birdfoot's Grampa" by Joseph Bruchac III. From ENTERING ONONDAGA by Joseph Bruchac. Reprinted with permission of Barbara S. Kouts. / "I Am" by Charmaine Bubenko reprinted by permission of the author. / "Eagerly" by Melanie Bubenko reprinted by permission of the author. / "My Six-line Poem" by Kerri Bugbee appeared in *Grade Nine Literary Anthology: Something to Believe In, 1990–91*. Graminia Community School. / "Untitled" by Arthur Buller appeared in *Punch*, Dec. 19, 1923. / "The Rhino" by Kirsty Butcher appeared in *The Last Rabbit: A Collection of Green Poems*, J. Curry, ed., Mammoth/Mandarin, 1990. / "Hero" by Mariah Carey. From the album *Music Box* by Mariah Carey. Sony Music Publishing, 1993. / "Mortality" by Tina Carlson reprinted by permission of the author. / "Hungry Ghost" by Debjani Chatterjee appeared in *Hearsay: Performance Poems Plus*, P. Beasley, ed., The Bodley Head, 1994. / "A Sailor's Love" by Erin E. Claussen reprinted by permission of the author. / "Monopoly" appeared in *John Robert Colombo Selected Poems* by John Robert Colombo, Black Moss Press, 1982. / "November" by Anne Corkett. From *Between Seasons*, Borealis Press, © 1981. Reprinted by permission. / "Wool Sweaters" by Eddie Craven reprinted by permission of the author. / "The Child Who Walks Backwards" from *The Garden Going on Without Us* by Lorna Crozier. Used by permission of the Canadian Publishers, McClelland & Stewart, Toronto. / "If a Poem Could Walk" from *Angels of Flesh, Angels of Silence* by Lorna Crozier. Used by permission of the Canadian Publishers, McClelland & Stewart, Toronto. / "pity this busy monster, manunkind" by e.e. cummings: Copyright 1944 by e.e. cummings, copyright 1972 by Nancy T. Andrews. Appeared in *Complete Poems 1913-1962* by e.e. cummings. Harcourt Brace Jovanovich, Inc. / "Hidden Beauty" by Heidi Ann Davidson reprinted by permission of the author. / "In My Backyard" by Celestino De Iuliis appeared in *Love's Sinning Song*, Canadian Centre for Italian Culture, 1981. / "Autumn Revenge" by Leyla Demir reprinted by permission of the author. / "How I Learned English" by Gregory Djanikian. From FALLING DEEPLY INTO AMERICA (Carnegie Mellon University Press) by Gregory Djanikian. Copyright © 1989 by Gregory Djanikian. / "A Dive" by Mary Jo Donnelly reprinted by permission of the author. / "Hair" by Kari-Lynn Dougherty reprinted by permission of the author. / "Tree" by Dominic Dowell appeared in *Does It Have To Rhyme?* by S. Brownjohn. Hodder and Stoughton, 1980. / "20th Century" by Louis Dudek appeared in *Small Perfect Things* by Louis Dudek. DC Books, 1991. / "A Case of Divorce" by Dwayne Edmundson reprinted by permission of the author. / "The Snake" by Richard Edwards appeared in *Wordplay: A Collection of Poems for Children*, BBC Educational Publishing, 1992. / "I shall" by Fouzi El-Asmar. From *The Wind-Driven Reed* by Fouzi El-Asmar. Reprinted by permission of Donald E. Herdeck, Publisher. / "Definition" by Matt Faulkner reprinted by permission of the author. Originally from Wolfville, N.S., Matt Faulkner now lives in Vancouver. / "Singing" by Matthew Festenstein appeared in *Does It Have To Rhyme?* by S. Brownjohn. Hodder and Stoughton, 1980. / "The Passenger Pigeon" by Paul Fleischman appeared in *The Place My Words Are Looking For*, P.B. Janeczko, ed., Bradbury Press, 1990. / "The Skaters" by John Gould Fletcher. From *Knock on a Star* by X.J. Kennedy and Dorothy M. Kennedy. Reprinted by permission of Little, Brown and Company. / "How

Much Does It Cost?" by Mary Fong appeared in *Home and Homeland*, P. Fanning and M. Goh, eds., Addison-Wesley Publishers Limited and Rubicon Publishing Inc., 1993. / "The Race" and "You May Now Kiss the Bride" by Kirsty Foot reprinted by permission of the author. / "I Wish I May, I Wish I Might" by Andrew J. Ford reprinted by permission of the author. / "From 'The Diary of a Young Girl'" by Anne Frank, trans. B.M. Mooyaard appeared in *The Works of Anne Frank* by Otto H. Frank. Doubleday, 1959. / "The Road Not Taken" by Robert Frost. From THE POETRY OF ROBERT FROST edited by Edward Connery Lathem. Copyright © 1956 by Robert Frost. Copyright 1928 © 1969 by Henry Holt and Co., Inc. Reprinted by permission of Henry Holt and Co., Inc. / "The Credo" by Robert Fulghum from ALL I REALLY NEED TO KNOW I LEARNED IN KINDERGARTEN by Robert Fulghum. Copyright © 1986, 1988 by Robert Fulghum. Reprinted by permission of Villard Books, a division of Random House, Inc. / "Bison" by Tonye Garter appeared in *Rising Voices*, A.B. Hirschfelder and B.R. Singer, eds., Ballantine Books, 1992. / "Prediction: School P.E." by Isabel Joshlin Glaser appeared in *Extra Innings: Baseball Poems*, L.B. Hopkins, ed., Harcourt Brace Jovanovich, 1993. / "Paul Hewitt" from CLASS DISMISSED II by Mel Glenn. Text copyright © 1986 by Mel Glenn. Reprinted by permission of Clarion Books/Houghton Mifflin Co. All rights reserved. / "All" by Leona Gom reprinted by permission of SONO NIS PRESS / "My Deaf Brother" by Phebe Graham reprinted by permission of the author. / "Gray" by Stephanie Gray reprinted by permission of the author. / "Friends" by Aaron Grenier reprinted by permission of the author. / "Wolves" by John Haines appeared in *A Book of Animal Poems*, W. Cole, ed., The Viking Press, 1973. / "Preposterous" by Jim Hall reprinted by permission of The University of Arkansas Press from *The Made Thing* by Leon Stokesbury, copyright 1982. / "First Love" by Joan A. Hamilton appeared in *Alberta Poetry Yearbook 1989/90*, J. Livingston, ed., Canadian Authors Association, Edmonton Branch. / "This Is Just To Say" by Allan Harms reprinted by permission of the author. / "Me" by Heather Harms reprinted by permission of the author. / "Those Winter Sundays" by Robert Hayden appeared in *Selected Poems* by Robert Hayden. October House, 1966. / "Mid-Term Break" by Seamus Heaney appeared in *Growing Up*, R. Jones, ed., Heinemann Educational. / "Cinquain" by Scott Hennig reprinted by permission of the author ('91 County of Parkland). / "Then" by Robert Hilles appeared in LOOK THE LOVELY ANIMAL SPEAKS. Turnstone Press Ltd. / "My City" by Kerra Hodges reprinted by permission of the author. / "This Is Just To Say" by Kristie Hodges reprinted by permission of the author. / "Foul Shot" by Edwin A. Hoey appeared in *Read* magazine, a Xerox Education Publication,

1962. / "Under the Beach Umbrella" by John Hollander appeared in *Types of Shape* by John Hollander. Atheneum, 1969. / "Who Am I?" by Felice Holman appeared in *Sound of Thunder*, I. Mills, ed., Addison-Wesley, 1993. / "The Photo" by Tara Holmes. From *The Claremont Review*, Number Five, Spring 1994. Terence Young, Susan Stenson, and Bill Stenson, eds., Reprinted by permission of the author. / "A Boy's Head" by Miroslav Holub appeared in *Involved in Poetry*, D. Scott, ed., Heinemann Educational, 1987. / "The Door" by Miroslav Holub appeared in *Selected Poems* by Miroslav Holub, translated by Ian Milner and George Theiner, 1967, translation copyright © Penguin Books, 1967. / "Early Supper" by Barbara Howes, copyright © 1956. From *Light and Dark* by Barbara Howes. Wesleyan University Press. Originally appeared in *The New Yorker*. / "Youth" by Langston Hughes appeared in *The Dream Keeper and Other Poems* by Langston Hughes. Alfred A. Knopf, Inc., 1932. / "Skiing Is," "Smash Time," and "Spinach" by Michael Janzen reprinted by permission of the author. / "Parents Just Don't Understand" by Jazzy Jeff & the Fresh Prince appeared in *Rap the Lyrics*, L.A. Stanley, ed., Penguin Books, 1992. / "Waiting" by Chasidy Karpiuk reprinted by permission of the author. / "I Grew Up" by Lenore Keeshig-Tobias, of the Nevaashiinigmiing reserve, appeared in *Seventh Generation: Contemporary Native Writing*, H. Hodgson, ed., Theytus Books. / "What We Might Be, What We Are" by X.J. Kennedy. Reprinted with permission of Margaret K. McElderry Books, an imprint of Simon & Schuster Children's Publishing Division, from GHASTLIES, GOOPS, & PINCUSHIONS by X.J. Kennedy. Copyright © 1989 by X.J. Kennedy. / "The Dragon Morning" by Samir Khalil reprinted by permission of the author. / "Elephants" by Patrick Lane appeared in *Patrick Lane: Selected Poems*. Oxford University Press, 1987. / "Ansel Adams's 'Moonrise'" by Julie Latham reprinted by permission of Joseph I. Tsujimoto. / "The Big Years" by Jo Lena appeared in *Poetry Alive: Perspectives*, D. Saliani, ed., Copp Clark Pitman Ltd., 1991. / "We Who Were Born" by Eiluned Lewis appeared in *Imagine Seeing You Here*, R. Charlesworth, ed., Oxford University Press, 1975. / "On Receiving My Driver's Licence" by Karmyn Lewis reprinted by permission of the author. / "Grey" by Cynthia Lim appeared in *B.C.E.T.A. Student Writing Journal*, 1993–94. BCETA, 1994. / "Niagara: Canadian Horseshoe Falls" by Myra Cohn Livingston. Reprinted with permission of Margaret K. McElderry Books, an imprint of Simon & Schuster Children's Publishing Division, from I NEVER TOLD AND OTHER POEMS by Myra Cohn Livingston. Copyright © 1992 by Myra Cohn Livingston. / "Long Beach: February" by Myra Cohn Livingston. Reprinted with permission of Margaret K. McElderry Books, an imprint of Simon